THE
WINNING
Spirit

BILL PENNINGTON

A BARBOUR BOOK

© 1991 by Bill Pennington

ISBN   1-55748-247-0

Quotations from *Out of the Blue*, published by Wolgemuth & Hyatt, Publishers, Inc., used by permission.

EVANGELICAL CHRISTIAN PUBLISHERS ASSOCIATION ᗍᎶᑭᗪ MEMBER

Published by   Barbour and Company, Inc.
              P.O. Box 719
              Uhrichsville, OH 44683

Typesetting by Typetronix, Inc., Cape Coral, Florida

Printed in the United States of America

*To Joyce, my best friend
and my best editor*

CONTENTS

◆ Contents ◆

v

◆ Acknowledgments ◆

This book is about baseball and people, though the two are one and the same anyway. The baseball community is just that, a community of dissimilar and yet alike people, wedded by a game that fosters a kinship and generosity of spirit.

I had a great deal of help from dozens working in this environment, beginning, of course, with the twelve athletes who provided their time to answer my questions and describe their stories. Friends, teammates, and family members helped flesh out the accounts greatly. They are wonderful people enjoying their lives, and there is real joy in knowing them.

This book could not have happened without the guidance, interest, and trust of Hugh Barbour, to whom I owe a great deal of thanks. Peter Golenbock deserves the very same thanks. Mike Celizic, too, gave a very important boost early on.

Stephen Reginald supervised the text from raw to ready, delivering it through the multitude of pressing details.

So many others assisted in materials gathered, access gained, telephone numbers acquired, and other various jump-starts when this book project seemed dead at one time or another. The following people graciously offered their help: Mike Kelly, Jim Wright, Tom Pedulla, Larry Schwartz, Steve Adamek, Dave Tilly, Don Burke, Rich Griffin of the Montreal Expos, Jeff Idelson of the New York Yankees, and the public relations staffs of the Los Angeles Dodgers, Houston Astros, and Pittsburgh Pirates.

Also, my appreciation to Tom Heitz and the amiable and efficient staff of The Baseball Hall of Fame Library in Cooperstown, New York. And a thank you to Gabe Buonauro and Rob Tanenbaum for their understanding along the way.

I will add that my wife, Joyce, literally labored through every moment of the manuscript with me. A gift beyond all others.

Finally, thanks to my parents, my brother, Don, and my sister, Linda, for staying up late at night to help write, edit, or type all my school papers from Sister Augustine on through Professor McLean. Everything that happened on Newton Street always seemed like it was out of a book anyway.

B.P.
WARWICK, N.Y.
MAY 1991

For what is a man profited, if he shall gain the whole world, and lose his own soul?

Matthew 16:26 (KJV)

JESSE
◆ Barfield ◆

1

When Jesse Barfield finally made the big leagues, he knew how to act. He had spent years practicing the swagger, the profanity, the aggressive self-promotion. In short, he had long ago learned what his peers expected: a boisterous, rambunctious locker room persona.

"To get along with the guys, you had to go along," Barfield says now, looking back on his debut season with the Toronto Blue Jays in 1982. "I had been getting ready for that process for at least five years and I jumped in with both feet. I did as they did."

It was a fairly all-consuming and greedy process. But Jesse had made it to the major leagues, achieving a lifelong goal, and now he wanted acceptance. He learned bad habits fast, and he was inventive, too.

"I had to do all sorts of things sometimes," he says. "For example, I hate the taste of beer but the guys all drank beer. So I'd take a beer, gut my way through a sip or two, and then when they weren't looking, I'd pour that beer out. They all thought I drank along with them."

Barfield says he wasn't really a bad guy in those years. He says he never used drugs, as did some of his teammates. But he still bought into a lifestyle he calls, "the young, immature pro athlete cut loose on the entire country."

Sometimes he calls it a "me" personality. Ask about his priorities then and he'll rank them: "Myself, money, and women."

"I thought I was enjoying myself," he says.

But always there was the disquieting stare of a teammate, Roy Lee Jackson.

Barfield liked Jackson, but something about Jackson troubled him. "He watched me and it was like he knew better," Jesse says. "Knew I wasn't really happy. And meanwhile, I used to watch him and be jealous. He had such peace. He was calm, an inner strength I wanted but I didn't understand.

"I found it very intriguing, but I didn't think about it much at first. I was too busy taking it all in. Taking a piece of this and a piece of that person without thinking much about giving anything back. Selfish-

2

ness is what it was."

Jackson saw something of himself in Barfield: a way of life he had lived before he was born again, before he accepted Jesus Christ into his life. Jackson watched Barfield from afar, and then he asked him to come to a Bible study.

"I wanted to be nice to Roy Lee, but I couldn't get away fast enough," Barfield says. "I ran from him, made up excuses. I was living what I thought was my dream come true, and I was going to keep running with this fun life."

That Barfield ever made it so far in baseball was a small miracle. He had been a noted, talented basketball player as a boy growing up in a fatherless household in a tough town, Joliet, Illinois. Barfield studied in school, longing for a college basketball scholarship. Hoops and the indoor game were going to be his way out of the poverty.

On a whim, he tried out for a local baseball club. A friend had insisted that he attend the tryout with him. Barfield said he'd go along to watch, thinking maybe he'd find a pick-up basketball game.

But Jesse Barfield did play some baseball that afternoon. He made the team and his friend didn't, a situation that changed when Barfield said he wouldn't play if his friend didn't get a uniform, too.

"I still don't know why I went that day,"
he says now. "It was a long way from my
house and no one had a car to drive me to
the practices. I rode my bike for miles. And
I never missed a practice."

Eventually Barfield tried out for, and
made, the high school baseball team. His
six-foot, 180-pound frame was deceptively
strong and wiry. He became a feared power
hitter, even if they only knew it in Joliet.

The baseball community of professional
scouts knew nothing of Barfield, the, basketball player turned outfielder. That
changed, however, when several scouts
came to a Joliet Central High School game
in 1977 to watch Bill Gullickson, the pitcher
for the visiting team.

Gullickson would make it to the major
leagues himself, but that day, he lost. In a
tense, close game, Jesse Barfield drove in
the game-winning runs with a double off
Gullickson. Now the baseball scouts had
contract offers for Barfield.

"I didn't know what to do," he says. "I
had been awarded a scholarship to study
architecture at Bradley University."

Jesse Barfield was seventeen years old, a
tough time to be making such decisions.
But the Toronto Blue Jays were offering
more money than anyone in the Barfield
home knew existed. So Barfield signed,
and in two weeks he was at the Blue Jays

Class A rookie farm team in Utica, New York.

He hit .206 with just two home runs in his first 441 at-bats. Jesse asked whoever would listen the same questions: "Did I blow it? Should I be at Bradley right now?"

His minor league manager, Denis Menke, suggested a weight-lifting program for the off-season. By 1981 at the Blue Jays top minor league team in Knoxville, Tennessee, Barfield had 16 home runs, 13 triples, and 24 doubles.

They knew about Jesse Barfield in baseball now. In 1982, he was handed the right fielder's job for the big club in Toronto. He summarily dropped it.

"I don't want to say I couldn't handle it or I wasn't ready because all young players in the major leagues start slowly," Barfield says. "But I was not an immediate success."

He knew how he was expected to greet such failure. "I swore a lot, kicked at things, tried to smash up water coolers," he says. "Those are all the things you're supposed to do. So I did them. Back then, baseball people said if you were committed to the game and truly dedicated, then you would go wild when things went right and wild when things went bad. It was almost a trained behavior."

Except for Roy Lee Jackson.

"When Roy Lee pitched, he was the same whether he gave up six runs or no runs," says. "He was an intense competitor; he tried very hard. He wanted to win, but he went about his job in such a different way. Here I was tearing things up and I had all this turmoil over my performance, and Roy Lee was calm, successful, and happy.

"He had a way about him that I had never seen before. It was an inner peace. I wanted what he had."

But not enough to go to church for it. "Roy Lee would start talking to me about Christ, but I always made excuses not to go," Barfield says. "I kept running from him. I had gone to church as a kid but I did that to please my mom. I always went and tried to keep from falling asleep.

"That's what church and Christ was to me. To me, to be a Christian meant that you were a pushover. Easy for tough guys like me."

So Barfield kept having his carefree fun. "It was never anything real bad, but it was that good-time life," he says. "Problem was, I had no defense for the highs and lows of baseball life, all the travel, the stress, the demands on your time, the competition."

Barfield pauses recalling the time. "The whole thing was wearing me down," he says. "It was getting harder and harder."

His live-in girlfriend—wife-to-be Marla—was pregnant with the couple's first child. Says Barfield: "It was all coming down around me."

Once again, Roy Lee Jackson was watching his teammate. He saw the turmoil. At last, Jesse Barfield and Marla accompanied Jackson to a Bible study.

"By the time we finished I had cried. I had this feeling like a great load was taken off my shoulders," Barfield says, "like a veil was taken off my eyes. Once we heard what the Bible was saying to us, there was no other choice. We accepted Jesus that night. Marla was filled with the Holy Spirit. It was June 23, 1982."

His conversion was immediate. Marla moved out to her own apartment (the two were married a short time later) and Jesse stopped using profanity. He did not throw tantrums when he struck out. Or at least he tried not to.

"He had times when he slipped," Marla Barfield says. "He wanted so much to be like Christ 100 percent of the time. It was hard at first. He'd get in a slump and have more trouble with things. But in the end, he made Christ number one in his life and everything was easier then." The transition, however, had its rough moments.

"I have to admit that some of my teammates were skeptical of my new life,"

Barfield says. "Christian athletes hear it all the time, that we are not going to be as aggressive. That we might be lackadaisical or too passive. I was anxious to prove that wrong. We all are. But I knew how people thought. Hey, I had been one of those people thinking the same way. It was important to dispel that notion right away."

It did not take Jesse Barfield long. Pivotal in this early mission was Yankees relief pitcher Rich Gossage. Nicknamed "Goose," Gossage was one of baseball's most fierce and feared competitors. A perennial All-Star, Gossage pitched for the then-dominant Yankees. His presence commanded. He would glare at hitters from the mound, daring them to hit his 95 mile-an-hour fastball.

Most often, they did not, Jesse Barfield included. Barfield came to the plate against Gossage not long after he was born again. He had no trouble recalling their last confrontation three weeks earlier.

"I had struck out on four pitches," he says. "I didn't come close to one pitch."

Facing Gossage after his conversion, Barfield said he felt strangely calm. "It had become a way of life for me," he says.

He singled off Gossage, driving in the game-winning run for the Blue Jays. When he faced Gossage two games later, he hit a game-winning home run.

The sportswriters who covered the Blue Jays wanted to know what had gotten into this new and improved Jesse Barfield. He was asked how he had found a way to beat Gossage at his own game, matching power with power.

"I used to be intimidated when I faced Goose," Barfield told the reporters. "Now I look forward to facing him. I look forward to the pressure in those situations."

As Toronto newspaper columnist John Robertson tells the story, Jesse then added: "I knew it would be a fastball and it was. I hit it square and I was afraid it would go foul. But the wind held it fair long enough, thank the Lord."

"You could see the jaws clench and the pencils pause in midair when Jesse said the word Lord," Robertson wrote in his column the next day. "Undaunted, Barfield added: 'I wish everyone could experience the things I've felt since I gave my life over to Christ.' "

Robertson went on to describe how Barfield talked to him afterward, saying: "Did you see the look on that one writer's face when I mentioned Christ? I know how he felt. I used to watch Roy Lee Jackson go through the same thing. But God has taken a tremendous weight off my shoulders; why shouldn't I be able to give Him the credit?"

That Robertson quoted Barfield exten-
sively on the subject of his strong religious
convictions was unusual. Most sports writers tend to leave such references out. It's
not brought up in postgame question-and-
answer sessions, nor used in the next day's
editions should a player give a version of
the events that includes a reference to
Jesus or to the Lord.

"It's something you just get used to,"
Barfield says. "Reporters, like some of
your teammates, call it Bible-thumping
when you do that. It doesn't stop me or
offend me. As I said, I understand what
they are thinking. I used to do it, too. It's
a part of my life, but I don't have to impart
it on theirs at all times.

"We all find our spots in this life. I want
others to be as happy as I am, but I can't
force them. What I can do is be there for
them like Roy Lee was for me. And I lead
my life in a way that shows them how
Christ can enhance a life. I try to be as
much like Him as I can and let others see
the wisdom in that from my behavior."

And Barfield, who was one of the American League's most prolific home run hitters in the late 1980s, has developed a
tremendous rapport with the bevy of reporters covering baseball in North America.
He has done so by showing respect. "I want
them to understand my situation and feel-

ings, so I do the same for them," he says.

One story involving Barfield and a female radio reporter speaks volumes to that end. It was 1988, and Suzyn Waldman was in her first few months working for WFAN in New York City. Following an important, late-season game between Toronto and the New York Yankees, Waldman was in the Toronto locker room attempting to get a postgame comment from Blue Jays outfielder George Bell.

Bell had been speaking to a group of reporters, but when Waldman arrived at the back of the pack, he burst into a blue tirade, screaming obscenities in both Spanish and English about a woman being in the locker room. Still screaming and gesturing, Bell said he would not continue the interview until Waldman left the room.

"It seemed like the entire locker room went silent," Waldman recalls. "I knew I had to leave and didn't want to make any more of a scene. I didn't want anyone to see me break down and cry. I was heading for the door, hoping could get out before I fell apart. I was almost there—the room was still quiet—when I heard a voice call out to me."

Said Jesse Barfield: "Hey, Suzyn. I went 3-for-4 today. Don't you want to talk to me?"

Waldman didn't know Barfield at the

time, though she later learned that he had turned to someone and asked for her name. She went to Barfield with her microphone and tape recorder and conducted the interview.

"He was terrific to me, even quoting some poetry," she says. "I've often wished I saved the interview because it represents one of the nicest things anyone has ever done for me. I was unnerved and upset and Jesse let me know it was OK, that I belonged. It was a beautiful thing to do for someone, especially someone he didn't even know. It showed genuine kindness."

"She was just trying to do her job, just like I am trying to do mine," Barfield says. "I only did what I'd want done for me. Is there any more basic rule of relationships on this earth?"

This attitude carries over to Barfield's relationships with other players. Two years almost to the day after his personal salvation, he noticed that his teammate Tony Fernandez was floundering.

"It is a very difficult life on the road as a baseball player," Barfield explains. "And there are many temptations."

"Jesse saw I was in need of spiritual help," Fernandez says. And just as Roy Lee Jackson had helped him, Jesse Barfield spent time with Fernandez.

"I talked to Tony about accepting Christ

into his life," Barfield says. "I told him He can save anyone. I had shown Tony for years how Christ had changed my life, given me a purpose. As I had watched Roy Lee lead his life with Christ and was impressed from afar, I think Tony had been watching me and felt the same way.

"We talked for a long time one day in the visiting locker room at Fenway Park in Boston." That day burns in Tony Fernandez's memory.

"It was June 24, 1984," Fernandez says. "Jesse and I got down on our knees and prayed in front of my locker right there in the Boston clubhouse. It changed my life. Without Jesse's insisting—and he wasn't pushy, he just knew I needed help—I don't know where I'd be as a person or a baseball player.

"I wouldn't be happy like I am now, because before I knew Christ I was very unhappy. I owe thanks to Jesse. I love him like a brother. He has a wonderful heart and compassion. He cares for people. That was what I noticed most in the past. I didn't understand how he could be so caring. Now I know that it can be done only by looking at Jesus."

Barfield completely agrees. "I have learned a love for people," he says. "Jesus does that for you. He created each person you look at in this world, so you know the love He has for them. It's so much easier to exist that way. Like everything else in my life since I accepted Christ."

And that includes his baseball career. "Oh, it's much easier to handle the ups and downs now," he says. "I think I've learned to always take the positive way because the negative ways in life are too easy. Five years ago, if you called me a no good so-and-so, we were going to have a fight right then and there. Now I don't have that desire. I understand where those kind of people are coming from, that they have a spiritual need.

"I feel the same way when I watch my teammates or opponents scream and kick things. I remember how I felt. I know what they're going through and it's not easy. I wish they could see how I see things now."

Barfield says his relationship with Christ also helped him through a situation he had never expected to encounter: meeting his father. The oldest of four children, Barfield had never known his father. His mother told him only that Dad had left home long ago.

"I didn't even know he was alive," he says. "I had wondered, but after all those years, you don't wonder anymore."

He was getting ready for a game against the California Angels in Anaheim in the summer of 1986 when he got a telephone call in his hotel room.

"This lady starts naming this cousin and that cousin and this uncle and telling me all about my family," Barfield remembers. "I figured she really knew my family. She wanted to meet with me, but I said I was kind of busy. She started telling me more about my family and me when I was little. I figured she really knew me, so I agreed to meet her.

"When I got together with her she said she had something to tell me. She said: 'I'm your grandmother.'

"I was stunned, I didn't know what to say. Then she told me something even more shocking. She knew my father, she knew he was alive and where he was. And, it turns out he is a man I had known as a boy.

"His name is Evelle Kelly. He was always a good friend of our family. He was always around the neighborhood in Joliet, helping out and looking out for the kids. She said he was my dad. I couldn't believe it. I called my mom, I guess she had her reasons for not telling me. I called Evelle on the phone. We talked. It was true."

Father and son got together in Detroit, where Kelly then lived. "It was strange at first," Barfield says. "Here was a guy I'd been around all my life and he was my father and I didn't know it. He does look like me, and he has an outgoing personality, like people say I do."

Reuniting with his father has made Barfield appreciate how important it is to establish a bond with his own children.

"The relationship between a father and a child is something I was deprived of," he says. "There are certain things you only want to talk about with a father, certain things you'd like to do with only a father, especially for a son. I try to remember that with my kids. Sometimes, like when I tell my son it's bedtime and to go upstairs and he says, 'But Daddy . . . ' three or four times, I have to remind myself that my son may want to talk. He may need to talk . . . .

"And yet, ten years ago, I wouldn't have been able to handle it this way. Not with maturity. It's Christ. I've tried to see things through His eyes and not my own. It has made such a difference. I would never have been able to be so happy with my dad, to go through meeting him, without Christ in my life. The knowledge that my Dad was alive and all the shock that came with that would have failed me somehow without Christ in my life. He showed me."

He has shown Jesse in other ways, too. Traded to the Yankees in 1989, Barfield had to adjust to playing in the United States, in the country's biggest city, and for a team noted for having a controversial locker room environment.

"You hear all the stories, but I was prepared to fit in and make peace," he says. "It was not difficult."

Noted for his calmness and level-headed demeanor in the unpredictable Yankees quarters, Barfield is well liked and admired by his teammates.

Said Dallas Green, his manager with the Yankees in 1989: "He is not only one of the most complete professionals in the game and a player who puts intense drive and dedication to his work ethic, but Jesse is someone who, most of all, should be emulated. People should know there are still people like Jesse in sports."

Somewhat modestly, Jesse Barfield agrees. "I loved playing in Toronto, but the one thing that bothered me was that we didn't get much publicity and attention because we played in Canada," he says. "I wanted to become better known because I'm proud of the person I am and the life I lead. I do not want to be an athlete who disappoints the public, especially kids. I try my best to live what I believe and be someone positive for them to look up to."

And if you want examples of how Jesse Barfield does that, wait outside Yankee Stadium after a home game. Barfield signs autographs for one and all, which often means a 45-minute postponement of his ride home.

"That's for the kids mostly," he says. "Kids need someone who cares and who is clean. Anyone can be tempted. Len Bias [the University of Maryland basketball star who died of a cocaine overdose] said he was a born-again Christian. I'll give him the benefit of the doubt on that. But I worry that he gave born-again Christians a bad name. You must stay with Christ because anything can happen if you step out of the boundaries.

"I know that without Christ, I felt empty and never had inner strength and peace. I did not have the compassion for people I have now. Accepting Christ and the inner strength I've received, has made me."

Now Jesse leads many of the chapel meetings held each Sunday at Yankee Stadium. "I enjoy it," he says. "I'm anxious to do that somewhere every Sunday, wherever I am in the country."

Barfield's travels continue during the off-season, when he makes public appearances. Often, he visits prison facilities.

"One of the largest gatherings was when I led a prayer service at the maximum security prison in Huntsville, Texas," he says. "I just want them to know someone cares. He is Jesus. He can help. And someone is there to help them find Him. Just as Roy Lee helped me."

Roy Lee Jackson is out of baseball these days, but Jesse Barfield carries on.

"It's like the bumper sticker I have," Barfield explains. "It says: 'You've tried everything else—now try God.' I did and I'm not ashamed to say it is the biggest part of my success, the best thing that ever happened to me, and the focus of a now happy life. It's simple: Try God."

TIM
◆ Burke ◆
2

Strange now, that Tim and Christine Burke could have ever considered their home so empty and their marriage so broken-hearted.

Today the Burkes are the parents of two daughters they adopted from Korea and a son from Guatemala. Their lives joyous and their home filled with love, Christine says the Burke family will grow.

"We have a big, beautiful house," she says of herself and husband, Tim, who now pitches for the New York Mets. "We might as well fill it up."

It is a goal Christine Burke could not have imagined on the day nine years ago when her belongings sat bundled by the door of the couple's apartment. Their life together had gone from trying and stormy to unbearable. Christine Burke had had enough.

"She was going to end the marriage," Tim Burke says. "Christine had packed up—bags at the door—and was ready to go. We had really hit bottom. People sometimes don't understand how you can so suddenly and desperately need the Lord's help in your life. Well, this is how it happens sometimes. It did to me."

It was 1982, and Burke was twenty-three years old. Now one of the National League's most dependable right-handed relievers, he was then a struggling minor leaguer playing in Buffalo. Rich Leggatt, a teammate who was a friend and former roommate, had become a Christian the previous year. For months, Leggatt had been encouraging Burke to join him at chapel or Bible study.

Tim Burke could not push his friend away nor deride him for his faith more quickly or more strenuously.

"I really treated him very badly," Burke says now. "It was awful when I look back at it. I was furious at him for changing. To me, he was always just reading the Bible. I'd get mad at him and yell at him. I'd say: 'You're wasting your life. You're a joke and no one believes you or what you're doing.'

"The previous year, Rich and I had been roommates and we used to go out constantly. We would hit the bars and hit the bottle. We drank a lot. I had developed a drinking problem that really had begun in college."

Burke had been a star at the University of Nebraska and would become a second-round draft choice of the Pittsburgh Pirates in 1980.

"Yeah, when I was at Nebraska I knew I was headed for a pro baseball career and it was a heady thing," Burke says. "I felt like I was going to be doing something I wanted, but I also got caught up in some behavior that seemed expected of pro athletes then. It was what I thought I was supposed to do: drink too much and hang around, living in bars.

"But the most damaging thing was the way I thought about the game. It became my god. Baseball was my life, and failure in this life meant baseball could end. The pressure if you think that way—that your life is baseball but baseball could fail you—was enormous. So to handle such stress, I drank a lot.

"When I married Christine, we started having problems almost immediately. It was because of my drinking and putting baseball number one. Everything was getting worse. I was pitching terribly, too. Looking back, I don't see how it could have been any different. I was falling to pieces in every direction imaginable. We were down low—low enough, finally, to listen to people I knew who had been trying to help us.

"Rich Leggatt and another teammate had asked me before to come to Bible study sessions with them. I had always told them to go away and leave me alone. I didn't want any part of it. They would be patient and talk to me about the Lord, but I didn't listen.

"As I said, the previous year, Rich had finally seen that the life he was leading in the bars and in the bottle had become too much for him. He asked the Lord for help. And afterward, as badly as I treated him then, he continued to care a lot for me and didn't get angry back. He said to me, 'I'm here for you if you need me.' He could see that I was in trouble. Anybody could just from watching me, but he really knew because he had been there.

"He knew that I was a mess. He kept asking me to come read the Bible with some of my other teammates. I refused over and over."

The sight of Christine's bags at the door moved something inside Tim Burke.

"I knew I had to do something, though I was wrestling with how I could justify it to myself," Tim says. "I mean, here I was refusing help one day and denying the Lord's ability to guide someone and then I go to a chapel meeting? I didn't know if I could do it. But when I saw that Christine was going to leave, well, things were just so bad. We had finally felt our need.

"I asked Christine if she would go to a Bible session with Rich. She agreed to go. I remember thinking, 'Well, we might as well; things can't get worse.' But I was skeptical to say the least. I didn't go there with hope."

But he did attend burdened. And he immediately felt a sense of relief at the gathering.

"The thing I remember most about that night was the peace I felt in the room the minute I walked in," Burke says. "My life was in such turmoil, and here there was such calmness. It was captivating. I wanted to feel that way so badly. It started to get better for me that day.

"I remember realizing that being a Christian wasn't just being a good person or a decent fellow. It was a relationship with Jesus Christ. It was letting Him in, accepting Him as number one in your life. It was realizing that He would accept you and guide you. I learned in that first session that being a Christian was letting Jesus in so He could forgive your sins. I realized I had never been forgiven my sins.

"So I kept going to meetings and reading the Bible, and about three months later . . . we both became Christians."

It was August 25, 1982.

"Jesus transformed my life in every way," Burke says now, speaking in a quiet and confident manner that belies none of the angst and turmoil his life and thoughts once were in. "He's given me the Holy Spirit to see life as He does, to guide me. He has taken a lot of pressure off me. In my profession, I don't worry about what the coaches are thinking or the manager or how my opponents are trying to unnerve me. I know the Lord is now in charge.

"The same goes for the rest of my life. I know not to let life's simple pleasures get away, and I know not to let little frustrations bother me. The Lord is in charge, and if I give my life over to Him, He'll guide me to good things . . . He has never made a mistake, and I don't think He's going to make His first one on me. Realizing that, everything changed."

The story of Tim Burke's professional life took a dramatic turn as well following his troubled season in 1982 at Buffalo. In his first two pro seasons, 1981 and 1982, Burke had compiled losing records: 8-10 in his first year and 7-10 the year after.

But in the spring of 1983, after an off-season trade from the Pittsburgh organization to the New York Yankees and an assignment to their minor league team in Nashville, Burke's career totals reversed.

He was a different pitcher, with an impressive 13-4 record and an ERA of 3.29.

The turnaround brought the notice of other major league teams. The philosophy of the Yankees franchise in that era was to deal its young talent for more established players and Burke was in demand following his season of success in 1983.

Montreal offered the Yankees a promising outfielder in Pat Rooney in December of 1983. The Yankees accepted. Rooney never did play in the major leagues. Burke, meanwhile, caught fire for the Montreal minor league teams.

Burke had another winning season in 1984, and followed it up with a record season in his first big league campaign with the Montreal Expos. He led the National League in games pitched, compiling a 9-4 record with eight saves. His ERA was an infinitesimal 2.39.

A nearly identical season of success as a middle reliever followed in 1988. And in 1987, now considered the ace and stopper in the Montreal bullpen, Burke was 7-0 with 18 saves and a 1.19 ERA.

"Naturally, any success, any turnaround I had in my career was related in every way to the day I accepted Christ into my life," Burke said while in Montreal. "For one thing, I lived a life that gave me a chance to perform to my abilities. My former lifestyle was killing me and my career. But more than that, any pressures on me that I was going to feel—on the field, on the road traveling, performing my job, handling the stress of being away from my family, whatever it is—He has made easier. As long as I live my life obedient to Him, He will guide me and give me the strength to overcome the distractions and the pressures.

"He gives me and all those who accept Him everything they need to lead their lives. On the road, my teammates and I have chapel sessions every Sunday and sometimes more often. And when we play at home, we have special gatherings. We'll bring in a local pastor and make the meetings for couples."

Burke's prowess as a late-inning reliever eventually earned him a position among the game's elite. He was feted in the United States and Canada after saving 84 games in four seasons from 1987 to 1990. But it was during the three-day, All-Star Game break in the 1989 major league season that he made news beyond anything gathered from his baseball accomplishments.

Tim and Christine Burke used the brief time off to fly to Guatemala to adopt their son, Ryan Richard. The story actually begins two years earlier, when the couple adopted their daughter, Stephanie Irene, in Korea.

"We had made a mission to Korea, but that's not when we adopted Stephanie," Burke says. "We later had to go back once all the paper work was completed. What had happened was that after a bunch of tests, it was determined that Christine and I couldn't have children unless the Lord did something miraculous.

"The Lord put the desire in our hearts to adopt a little Korean girl. So we did. A few years later, the Lord gave us the desire to adopt a child that didn't have a home. It was in our hearts to have another child, and it turned out to be a little boy from Guatemala. They are real joys. They have fit into the family perfectly."

The Burkes adopted a third child in May 1991, Nicole, also from Korea.

But it was the Burkes' trip to Guatemala, coming as it did during the 1989 All-Star break, that struck a chord in the international press, bringing reporters to Montreal to tell the Burke family's story for months afterward.

"I never seek that kind of publicity, but since it came along, I can see the positives in it," Tim Burke says. "I'll tell you why. We have received hundreds of letters, hundreds and hundreds of letters, from people who were trying to adopt and didn't know what to do. Or had been trying to adopt but in this country only and hadn't thought of trying a different way.

"There are people who hadn't thought about all the kids without homes throughout the world who need help. The story of our situation and the publicity surrounding it has helped quite a few children without homes to get adopted. As I see it, the Lord has used it in that way."

Some would also say that the publicity Burke received during the 1989 All-Star Game break helped cast a kinder light on the Christian baseball player at a time when it was needed. It was a season when several daily newspapers focused on the difficulties some Christian athletes were facing in their efforts to be accepted.

"I don't know what role I've had in it, but I think there's no question that we are more accepted these days than before," Burke says. "People know more about Christian athletes and are more comfortable and familiar. There still are stereotypes—people who think, 'Oh, he's a born-again Christian so he doesn't care if he wins or loses. He doesn't work hard and he isn't aggressive.'

"But there's a lot less of that because it's so ridiculous. If Jesus were on the field, He'd be breaking up double plays. He'd be high-fiving the other guys. That's what Christianity is supposed to be. Some people lose their fire, but not because of the Lord.

We are not wimps. We are aggressive ball-players and we do care about winning and we work hard.

"It has helped that some spotlighted players recently have been Christians. Guys like Orel Hershiser when he had that phenomenal season in 1988 and Brett Butler in the 1989 playoffs and World Series. That has helped people to understand, and I think most everyone now realizes that Christian players are out there to win and try hard just like everyone else. The Lord wants us to try as hard as we can, to give everything we have to an effort. He wants us to work and He preaches that to us in the Bible."

In a very general way, Burke sees his fame as useful. "Part of our job as Christians is to live our lives in a godly manner," he says. "And in the sense that people see that and realize there is a peace there—as I did when I attended my first Bible session—that is good. And yet, the fact is don't follow me or Orel Hershiser; follow Jesus. We certainly are not perfect people. We are making struggles all the time. But the Lord will guide us through because we have accepted Him in.

"Still, I have to realize that there's no question we as baseball players have been given quite a platform. Every professional athlete has, not just those who are Christians. There's no doubt that we can influence people's lives.

I don't seek that, but if I am going to influence people, then I want to influence them in a positive way.

"That's how I look at it. Not just letting them see a Christian lifestyle, but even from a moral aspect. Let's help kids see how someone leads a good and moral life and let that be a positive that comes from fame."

To Tim Burke's mind, it all has to do with perceptions.

"Going back to that season in 1982, I certainly had my impressions and understanding of my Christian friends all wrong," he says. "But I saw their peace. I saw it even though I tried not to. And now there are people who think of Christians and think of soap boxes, of preaching on the street about going to hell. I don't preach to my teammates. It is our walk with Christ that matters. Our walk is far more important than going up and preaching at somebody."

BRETT
◆ Butler ◆
3

Brett Butler figured he had it all: a career that brought riches and attention, a loving family, and the confidence that he controlled all in his domain.

"I had everything working my way," he says. "I was on top of the world. My family life was fine. I had just signed a nice, big contract. I was a Christian, but I was always thinking that I was going to do things my way. Hey, everything was going my way."

The 1985 baseball season had just ended, a breakthrough year professionally for Butler. In his second year with the Cleveland Indians, Butler had been among the American League leaders with a .311 batting average. He had led all major league outfielders in fielding percentage.

"The best year of my career," Butler, who

now plays for the Los Angeles Dodgers, says. "I was feeling so great about myself. I think there are times when as believers we take God, and we put him in our back pocket. That's what I did. And I think there are times like that time in my life when God spanks us as a father does a child who needs to be corrected."

Butler felt the jolt directly.

"I was struck by God and I was saved by a miracle," he says. "And it was all for my benefit.

"I was playing racquetball with a friend after the 1985 season. I had glasses on. He hit a forehand, and as I turned to see it, I was hit right in the glass around my right eye. Right off the racquet.

"The glass shattered around my right eye and put me in the hospital for six days with both eyes patched. The doctors gave me a 50-50 chance of getting the sight back in my right eye and a very slim chance of having my eye to the point of where it was before the injury.

"I remember lying there and I said: 'Lord, I have accepted You into my life as my Savior, but truthfully, there is one thing that I have never done.' I guess in a sense I always knew that baseball was a god to me because deep down that is all I lived to do—play baseball. And I remember fighting this battle between God and baseball and what I wanted to do.

"In that hospital bed I had so much time to think with those patches on my eyes, and I realized if God loves me so much that He sent His only Son, then He knows I love the game as much as I do. And I knew that He wouldn't do anything to hurt me. He won't take baseball away from me unless it's what I need to have done.

"So I remember lying there and I said: 'Lord, You said that You'd take care of me no matter what. If it's Your will for me to continue to play the game, You can claim the fame. Because You've made me. You will have healed my eye and made me the kind of player that I am. But if not, and You arrange for me to do something else, be a car salesman or a teacher, whatever, then I'll accept that because I know that You'll have a perfect plan for my life.'

"And I got a peace that said: 'I'll take care of you—whatever it may be.'

In the succeeding days, Butler's doctors remained unsure of how the right eye would heal. The most optimistic of them predicted that Butler had a 70 percent chance of regaining his sight in it.

"I was unworried," Butler says now, smiling through eyes that know the end of the story. "The fact is, my right eye had always had 20-20 vision but I had had an astigmatism. As I recovered at home, the

eye kept improving. Six weeks before I
went to spring training in 1986, I had a test
on my eye. The vision in my right eye was
20-15 and the astigmatism was gone. My
eye was better than it was before. My only
response was, it's a miracle of God that
allowed me to understand what He was
trying to do. He was saying, 'Let Me control your life, not you.'

"Since then, I've given God the game. It
wasn't easy for me, but I had to look at it
and see that all along He was definitely
steering my career. If God could take a 5-
foot-9-inch, 160-pound athlete and let him
be successful in the big leagues, that's a
miracle in itself. I mean, I didn't even start
on my high school team.

"But God has made it work for me. Even
if I did need Him to humble me back in '85.
As long as we can learn from our mistakes,
we can grow and we can strive to be the
kind of people God wants us to be. Back
then, it was just His way of saying: 'Hey,
remember, I'm the one in control, not you.' "

Butler's baseball milestones have had a
way of focusing his priorities throughout
his career.

In 1981, for example, Butler finally broke
through to the major leagues. An odyssey
spanning five years and 326 minor league
games concluded with a start in center
field for the Atlanta Braves.

"I remember the game so well," he says. "I remember getting my first hit, driving in a run and scoring one, too. I remember the winning. I remember the reporters at the end of the game. Everything was exactly how I had thought it would be. I had dreamed of it for so long.

"I went back to my hotel room that night and I cried. I said: 'Is this all there is to it?' Here was my dream—to get to the big leagues—and now I'm in the big leagues and all I think of is that there must be something else. Something more.

"Once again, I said to the Lord: 'I see that You are the only thing that can fill the void in my life.' It can't be the materialistic things in the world. And I can honestly say that I remember calling my wife, who was then my fiancée, and I told her how unfulfilled I felt. Here I've finally reached my dream and it's so empty. So shallow. Not lasting.

"But I knew that a personal relationship with God will last for eternity. Nothing else much matters. I only wish I had learned the lesson earlier. I wouldn't have wasted so many of those years."

In the earliest portions of Butler's life as his baseball success was burgeoning, he struggled to understand his vocation and the bizarre lifestyle it seemed to lead him through.

"It wasn't just the road a minor league baseball player travels, it was the road that I was on," he says. "I know that the road that I was on, with the drinking, and the chasing and everything else, would have led me to a road of destruction.

"There are a lot of people who on the outside look like they're having a great time but on the inside they're miserable. There's a void in their life and that void is God. I believe that. I went through all that."

Butler's conversion, as is often the case, was not immediate, even after he had realized how greatly he needed to change his life.

"My acceptance of Christ took steps," he says. "I guess it was the way it was always going to work for me. I guess we all get the message in different ways. I remember that the first step was when I went to a Fellowship of Christian Athletes conference in Fort Collins, Colorado, in 1973.

"To me, I had accepted Christ in my life at that time. I felt that I had been brought up in a Christian home. We attended church. But accepting Christ as my Savior? Well, I was more a head Christian than a heart Christian. The main difference was that I believed in God, I understood God, but I didn't accept Him into my life as the controller and the Savior of my life.

"I had somebody ask me a question at that conference: 'If I was to die did I know I'd go to heaven?' I couldn't answer definitively yes or no. I figured I was a pretty good guy, maybe I would. But I wanted to be sure that I was going to heaven by asking Christ into my life.

"There are a lot of people who say they have done that, but it's a personal relationship . . . . The difference is God knows your heart and that's the personal relationship of being born again, born of the Spirit.

"I thought I had accepted Christ as my Savior. I thought I had done what I truly needed to."

But as smart as Butler thought he was being, in his heart, he knew he was treating his relationship with Christ as just another game in his contest-filled life.

"From 1973 when I attended that conference probably until 1981 when I met my wife, I tried in my own way to sift the things that I thought were what God wanted me to do," Butler says. "I wasn't a big drinker but I smoked a little grass. I did some of the things that as a Christian I can't do. But more than anything else, there was one thing that I could not give up. I was a winer-diner, and if it led to anything, I didn't think it was any big deal. I was a Christian, but I was trying to do it my way instead of God's way. I would wake up in the morning after a one-night stand, and I'd have a guilty conscience.

"I knew that I was living in sin. I knew that it was wrong—I finally got on my knees and said: 'Lord, I've sifted the drinking; I've sifted the cussing and all the problems I've caused. But Father, the one thing I can't give up is the women. I give up the situation to you Father. I ask you to put a Christian woman in my life to take the desires of the flesh away.'

"And in 1981 I met my wife in Richmond, Virginia, where I was playing for the Braves AAA affiliate. After the third date I knew that God had just come into my heart and I knew that she was the one for me. I told her, 'You're going to think I'm crazy but I feel that God has put you into my life.' Ironically enough, her comment to me was that just four weeks prior to that she had accepted Christ and asked God to put a Christian man in her life.

"Of course, the desires were still there at times. I think as Christians when we ask Christ into our lives He gives us the strength to handle adversity. There are times when desires of the flesh come, but getting into the Word, having fellowship with other believers, going to a solid church, and being involved with godly people helps you to suppress those desires and live the kind of life God wants you to.

"It's a chosen thing. I don't drink anymore, or very seldom. I may have a glass of wine at dinner with my wife. I don't smoke. I don't chase women. I don't do any of that anymore. Because those are not the ways of God. When you're not a Christian, you know it's wrong but you still do it. When you have the Spirit in your life, then it suppresses you so you know that it is not a thing a Christian should do. And as much as maybe the flesh might want to do it, you don't do it. It is really a fight between the Spirit and the flesh of the person.

"It's a constant battle, a constant fight knowing that Satan is a part of our life. Satan is real. And it's a fight with Satan more than anything else.

"But God's Spirit gives me direction. I've been in situations where there have been women and if I had wanted to I could . . . and God says flee from the temptations. I am a human being. So I run. I go back and I call my wife and I tell her how much I love her.

"In every way possible, you can't imagine how much calmer, peaceful, and productive Christ has made every facet of my life."

Baseball fans relish the evidence. Combining speed with a tenacious presence at the plate, Butler has become one of the

game's best leadoff hitters. In his four
seasons at Cleveland, Butler batted .288,
leading the American League in triples
twice. In that same period, he walked 310
times and stole 164 bases.

After the 1987 season, Butler signed a
free agent contract with the San Francisco
Giants, helping to lead the Giants to the
World Series in 1989. Declared a free agent
again after the 1990 season, Butler landed
in Los Angeles, teamed with a fellow Christian he has long admired: Orel Hershiser.

"It's a dream place to play," Butler says
of his new locale. "I have put my trust in
the Lord and he has never let me down. It
has been so much easier to live my life and
enjoy my life, it amazes me every day.

"I do not know how an unbeliever can
handle life. The ups and downs, the depression without having God. For me now,
there are no ups and downs. God is my
stabilizer. He's my strength when I'm
down. He's my fortress to lean on when
things are going bad. He's my joy when
things are going good and I thank Him for
the blessings. If I could pick things I wanted
in my life—my wife, my four beautiful
kids, more money than I ever dreamed of
having—I couldn't have picked the life I
have now. And I know that everything I
have now is a gift from God.

"It's not by my good works, but by His

grace, His mercy, which I marvel at. I have children and you have to sit back and say: 'Would I give one of my four kids up for anybody in this room or even give up one of my kids for my wife?' I don't think I would do that. But God loved us so much that He gave up His only Son for us. So that if all we do is believe, we have everlasting life.

"It's so simple, really. Read the Bible. God said there are those that are going to believe and there are those that aren't. There are those that are going to heaven and there are those that are going to hell. But it's our free choice. And either we choose to accept Him and follow His way or we choose not to. God never said that we are not going to go through hard times. But God gives me the strength to handle the hard times. He gives me the joy to handle the good times. He's in control. He is going to be there for the good. He is going to be there for the bad. And He is never going to leave me.

"And I know that when my time comes, when it's time for Brett Butler to leave the earth, Brett has got a place to go. I know I'm going to heaven. There are no ifs, buts or maybes. People that aren't believers don't have that assurance. They say, 'Yeah, when I die, it will be no big deal.' But God talks about eternity as being a long time and I want to have that.

"My father died in 1984. He was forty-nine years old and in perfect health. I remember coming home one day after having a dream that he died. I said: 'Dad, I gotta ask you something. If you died would you go to heaven?' And he said: 'Yes, son, I will.' I asked him how he knew and he said: 'Because I asked Christ into my heart.' "

Butler does not shy away from using his position as a professional athlete constantly in the public eye to set an example of a life walking with Christ.

"Not at all," he says. "It's my responsibility from the plateau that I am put on as a major league player to try to influence as many as I possibly can for the kingdom of God. What I try to do is speak to youth. I speak to adults, too. If the opportunity is brought up to me to share the Gospel I do that—as much as I possibly can. Not so much to Bible pound, but to say that this is the way it is. This is the way God tells it. This is His Word. Either accept it or you reject it.

"I don't want to push myself on others. I've had a hard enough time trying to take care of my own family and myself to be persecuting and getting on other people. But if I can be a positive influence, maybe they will answer the same question I once had to: 'If I was to die would I go to heaven?'

"I do this and I play baseball to the best of my ability because that's what God has given me. I do this even though I am torn between this life and the life God talks about as a far better place in heaven. I'm torn between having the game of baseball, my wife, and my family, and wanting to go home to God. The most important thing in my life is my relationship with God. My family comes second and then the game and everything else after that.

"Lately, so many people ask me what I want to do when baseball is over and I say that I want to be the kind of father and husband that I need to be. I've said before that I've wanted to manage a major league baseball team. I've said I wanted to be a general manager of a team. I've wanted to go into broadcasting.

"I don't know. Lately I've been thinking that maybe I'll stay home and be 'Mr. Mom.' I'll try to raise my kids in a Christian home. I'll try to raise them the way God wants me to. Maybe that is the best thing I can do."

GLENN
◆ Davis ◆
4

What Glenn Davis has become is what his
mother, Margaret, feared most: a baseball
player.

What baseball has become for Glenn Davis
is what Margaret Davis sought for him: a
pulpit.

What has become of Glenn Davis is something Margaret Davis would have never
thought possible: a nationally known, oft-
told story of Christ touching a life.

It never figured to be this way. Glenn and
Margaret Davis certainly never saw it coming. Not this way, not through baseball.

To Margaret Davis, baseball was at the
root of a lot of wrongdoing.

And for much of his early life, Glenn
Davis, now the power-hitting star of the
Baltimore Orioles, went about proving it.
Just as his father, Gene, had a generation

before.

Ten years in baseball's minor leagues, Gene Davis bounced around the country. Developing what was a powerful swing at the plate, he also developed a powerful drinking problem.

It's not uncommon. The minor leagues are a life of nightlong bus rides and games played in countless little towns where the vagabond ballplayer is at worst unwelcome, at best a summer visitor, and always foreign to the year-round cares and concerns of the community.

It's easy to feel lost in these surroundings: away from your old home, and yet never truly a part of your new one.

This nomadic life can include promotions and demotions within a given team's minor league system. Like company transfers, they come yearly and sometimes monthly.

Like many before him, Gene Davis found this lifestyle difficult. He struggled to rise above it, raising a family in Jacksonville, Florida, as he pursued his baseball dreams, but by his own admission, he failed.

"There's failure in every part of life," says Gene Davis, now a post office manager in Jacksonville. "But I did not handle it well. When I was playing ball, I was drinking. I was not honest. I'm not proud of it. I know it hurt my family dearly.

"Eventually, I decided it would be best if

I just left, left them alone. Left town."

That was when Glenn Davis was seven, more than old enough to know that his early homelife had not been like others. When his father was around—which was not often—there had been constant fighting between his parents. When his father was off playing baseball, Davis sought recreation and companionship in town-sponsored athletics. Growing up in Jacksonville, he was always one of the best at whatever game was being played, especially baseball. But even in this arena where he excelled, he was different.

"All the other boys had fathers taking them back and forth to games and working with them," Davis says. "I was always alone. A young boy needs a father to listen about his successes, to comfort in the failures, to praise and nurture. I was alone."

Davis reacted by developing a defiant attitude.

"I had a chip on my shoulder," he says. "I looked for fights. I was big and strong, but kind of a chunky kid. When other kids called me Fatso, I used to kill half of them."

When his father and mother separated, things did not improve for Davis.

His mother was determined to keep him out of sports, for fear that he would follow his father's path.

"I know what goes on in professional

sports, having been through it once before," she told *Sports Illustrated* when the
magazine did a profile of her son in 1987.
"It is what I feared most for Glenn."

But sports held an allure for Davis. They
offered an identity; it was what he did best.
Margaret and Davis clashed. She decided
that he was to become a minister of their
church, and as part of that decision, she
prohibited her son from hanging around
the playground. Behind her back, Davis
played baseball.

And so began another tortuous piece of
Davis's life. It was a hypocritical stage.
Margaret Davis tried to instill Christian
values with regular Sunday church visits
and readings from the Bible. Davis played
the dutiful son, but it was always just
that—something he played.

"I knew every sermon, every Scripture
reading," he says. "I was admired by the
elders at the church. I was there waiting
when the doors were opened every Sunday
and on Wednesday nights, too. I knew
every lesson by heart. I could quote the
Bible from Genesis to Revelation.

"But there was a real me and a fake me.
I had the people at the church fooled. I had
them all fooled."

The real Glenn Davis was desperate, depressed, even suicidal. He felt his life was
a sham. He believed none of the sacred

words he uttered. He felt alone in the world, aimless, unloved.

Many nights Davis would return to his mother's home, go to his bedroom and sit with a .25 caliber pistol he kept in the top of his dresser. Sometimes he would load it, sometimes not. But always, he played with it, pointing it at his head and imagining what it would be like to end his unhappy life.

"I would put the gun to my head unloaded and squeeze the trigger over and over," he says. "I lay there for an hour doing it. I felt like my mother and father had caused all my unhappiness and my uncertain life. I thought maybe if I killed myself it would hurt them.

"All through my teenage years I constantly thought about committing suicide. I held knives to my stomach and thought about stabbing myself. I thought about running into the street in front of a car. But ultimately, I could never do it.

"I felt like an ugly duckling, unloved and alone in the world. I sat in my room and cried to God, asking Him why He was letting all these things happen to me. I realize now that I was feeling sorry for myself, but at the time, I just felt like nobody loved me, nobody cared about me. I felt like I had nothing. I didn't have a mother or a father. I guess I ruined my family, or so I thought.

"I thought maybe I was the reason my parents split up. My mother wouldn't let me see my father or his family. I used to sneak out to meet him and everyone in the neighborhood made fun of me for doing it, sneaking out of the house and down to the corner to meet my own father.

"It infuriated my mother and she would punish me. In return, I would refuse to see any of her family. The result was that I had no one. I was confused and feeling sorry for myself, too. Worst of all, I never saw all the wrong I was doing to myself and others."

There were the fights.

"I used to hang around in town and pick fights," he says. "I'd pick fights for no reason at all with whoever I thought would fight back. Or I'd just beat on someone smaller than me. I loved to fight. I never did take anyone's life but I came close a couple of times."

Fighting was not his only illegal activity. He broke into some cars, vandalized others. He drank, he smoked, he cursed, he caroused. He was nearly banned from the Jacksonville school system when he punched his elementary school principal in the face.

Says Davis: "People told me there was something wrong with me. I laughed at them, even though I knew they were right.

At fifteen years old, I was your basic juvenile delinquent heading for prison."

He was also the ultimate con man. Asked why he was never arrested in Jacksonville, Davis replies: "I had a knack for quoting the Scriptures the minute a police cruiser showed up. I knew when to turn it on, to act like the good Christian schoolboy when the trouble I had started got out of hand."

Not everyone was fooled.

Margaret Davis knew her son was out causing havoc on the streets almost nightly. But she says she did not know how to react. There were beatings and other forms of the most severe punishment.

The despair of parent and child did not subside.

"I wanted to die all that much more," Davis says. "I felt like I was living in hell. I knew all my bad deeds were going to make me pay someday and I just wanted it to end."

"I knew Glenn had many struggles," Margaret Davis said in the *Sports Illustrated* interview. "I wasn't the perfect mother, but then Glenn was a headstrong boy and I felt I had to apply some discipline."

Gene Davis believes it was a no-win situation for everyone concerned. "I think Margaret was trying to be the father Glenn never had," he says.

His abilities as an athlete kept Glenn

Davis in school. At University Christian High School, he teamed with friend Storm Davis, a schoolboy star then and now a pitcher for the Kansas City Royals. Together, the two led University Christian to back-to-back state baseball championships.

"It was the only time I was happy," Davis says.

To play ball, Davis had to stay relatively trouble-free during school hours at least. He toned down his hooliganism inside the classroom and graduated from University Christian.

But when the structure of school and its attending athletic programs vanished, Davis floundered again. The clashes with his mother intensified. He moved out of the house for days on end, sleeping on park benches.

He lived by stealing and mowing lawns in Jacksonville.

"Sometimes I think I must have mowed every blade of grass in the city at one time or another that summer," he says.

At the end of the summer, Davis's life took a dramatic turn, the first steps of a four-year journey that led him to life with Christ. Removing his last belongings from the Tulsa Road home where his mother lived and he had been raised, he moved into the house of his old classmate, Storm Davis.

Though the two families are not related, it made the transition easier that they shared the same name. Besides, the two boys had grown close. Storm's parents, George and Norma Davis, virtually adopted their son's friend.

"He had been out on his own, ruining his life," Norma Davis says. "We accepted him into our lives and our home."

"It was a new lesson in love for me," Glenn Davis says. "They were religious, too, but that's not something I paid attention to immediately. What I noticed most was the difference in lives and homes. They were a complete family, something I had never had.

"I guess I caused many of my own problems but they were beginning to show me what love was all about. I knew my mother tried in her way, but George and Norma got through to me in some little ways."

But not in every way. Davis had been a con man too long. He continued to con the world—or so he thought—he just did so from a far more stable base of operations.

"We knew he practically lived in bars and slept around a lot," says Norma Davis. "I had to fight the girls off the phone."

Eventually, Davis attended the University of Georgia on a baseball scholarship that he could not keep. He transferred to Manatee Junior College in Bradenton,

Florida, where the Houston Astros spotted his powerful swing and made him a secondary phase draft pick in 1981.

Davis received a $25,000 signing bonus. He spent it all in six months. Assigned to the Astros minor league team in Daytona Beach, Davis began reenacting the destructive lifestyle his father had followed years before him.

"When you think about it there's almost something eerie about how our lives paralleled," he says.

He used the money from his first contract to buy a condominium overlooking a golf course, a Trans Am sports car, and a lot of drinks in a lot of bars. He also funded countless parties at his condo.

"I was living fast and furious, heading for the worst places all over again, just in different cities and in a newer, faster car," he says. "My life was drinking and impressing women. Any way I could use someone, I would. I was going to end up dead or in jail."

In 1982, his second pro season, Davis excelled, batting .315. He tied for the league lead in home runs with 19. It should have been a heady time for the twenty-two year old.

"But the things I was doing had no meaning," he says. "I wasn't having any fun. I was playing well, but my life was in chaos so what good was it? I used to say to myself all the time, will I ever find peace and happiness?"

Davis says now that it was probably the most disconcerting time of his life, which considering all he had already experienced, says a lot.

"I was doing all these things that I thought would give me happiness. I had baseball and money, too, but it wasn't enough. It scared me to death."

And again, death entered his mind. He wondered: Given the chance, would he pull the trigger this time?

Before the 1982 season ended, the Daytona Beach team held a team chapel meeting. The subject was hypocrisy. Davis, as he always did, thought the topic appropriate. Still, it was only a thought, at best the seed of what was to follow.

Glenn Davis returned to Jacksonville that fall, to the home of George and Norma Davis—a couple he now called Mom and Dad. He was still driving the Trans Am literally and figuratively full-speed through life.

One afternoon, he came up behind Norma Davis and greeted her merrily with a smile and a "Hi, Mom!"

"I'm not sure I want you to call me Mom anymore," she answered. "You're not fooling anyone with your life . We know how you spend your nights and what you are doing with your money and your time. No son of mine would act that way, treat other people that way."

Davis was stunned, shaken, disbelieving.

"We've been trying to be mother and father to you," Norma continued. "We've shown you the way and all you've done is make a joke of it. You can stay here, you'll always have a bed to sleep in if you want one, but we've quit being your mother and father."

"I felt like a complete ruin," Glenn Davis remembers. "I was ashamed. I knew she was so right. I started crying and I couldn't stop. I went out onto the front stoop and just fell to my knees."

Norma Davis came out to join him.

"I told her my life was in ruins, confusion. I told her I needed help," he says.

Norma dropped to her knees next to the troubled young man and the two prayed.

"Norma started telling me how Jesus can save people if they ask for His help. I looked up and asked God to save me," Davis says. "I said, if what they say is true, that Your Son can save me, then do it right now or I'm going to kill myself.

"I immediately stopped crying, the tears just stopped. I felt complete relief. That chip I had on my shoulder for all those years was gone. It is the day I realized life could be good and worthy.

"September 15, 1982, I'll never forget that day."

In the years since, Glenn Davis's life has been so transformed, it's hard to see anything resembling the irreverent adolescent and angry, aimless young man he describes when asked about his difficult struggle before he found Christ.

He is soft-spoken, humble and quiet. Before being acquired by Baltimore this winter, he had spent six seasons with the Houston Astros, where he was considered the consummate teammate.

"There's an evenness to his personality that helps everyone's mood," says Baseball Hall of Famer Yogi Berra, who was an Astros coach from 1986 to 1989.

In keeping with his reputation, Berra cut to the point in his unique, well-documented way: "Happiness makes everyone happy."

Happiness followed Glenn's 1982 redemption in steps. In the summer of 1983, playing at the Astros' AA minor league level in Columbus, Georgia, he again tied for the league lead in homers with 25 and he batted .299.

While his baseball star was rising, his personal life was coming together joyously. He met his wife-to-be, Teresa Beesley. They were married in 1984, the year Davis broke into the big leagues.

"Teresa brought a tremendous stability to my life," he says. "Now, this is a family life. A real family life."

The two are nearly inseparable. Glenn's Houston teammates used to refer to Teresa as "American Express." Why? Because Glenn never leaves home without her.

With Teresa's help, Glenn has also set about reestablishing his ties with his birth mother and father.

The first step was getting everyone together for the 1984 wedding. With Norma and George Davis, Glenn's mother, who had remarried and was now Margaret Todd; and Gene Davis and his second wife, it was a confusing collection for Teresa's family.

"It was a beginning," Davis says, smiling at the thought.

Margaret Davis still wishes her son had become a preacher and she is not happy with all phases of his stardom, but she is proud of his accomplishments and recognizes how his life story and its prominence in the national media—a movie of his life is still in the planning—has spread the word of Jesus Christ.

"Our relationship is not typical of the son-and-mother relationship most know," Davis says. "But the Lord is bringing us together. There is love. We have been through so much. I call her and send her cards on her birthday, which is something I never used to do.

"My father and I write letters and talk, too. That makes me feel good."

Davis's career as one of the most feared sluggers in the National League was, of course, a source of pride to many in the Houston area as well. He did not, however, let fame and notoriety alter his Christian convictions.

There was, for example, the fight Davis put up over a beer promotion that followed his home runs on the Astros television broadcasts. Like many teams, the Astros television network had a paid commercial endorsement announcement after each homer by a Houston player.

After Davis's home runs, an announcer would proclaim: "Glenn Davis, this Bud's for you!"

Davis protested. Other Christian athletes followed suit in other cities, led by his example.

"I couldn't very well let that go by," he says. "It's not something I stand for, how could I?"

Traveling the country the past five years, Davis has often been asked to recount his story of struggle and ultimate success. How Christ saved him from sure destruction.

"Sometimes I tire of the interviews," he says. "I was saying just that the other day [to Norma Davis], that I'm no one special, so why do they want my story? She told me to remember who I was and what I went through. She asked me if fame is harder than poverty."

And occasionally in his baseball life, there has been what Glenn calls a "God incident." For example, when he hit his fifteenth home run in the 1985 season, breaking the Astros record for home runs by a rookie, he did so on September 15, the third anniversary of his salvation.

"That's more than a simple twist of fate," he says. "Think about it."

Glenn Davis often sees his life in such "God incidents."

"It seems like my life has been a crossword puzzle," he said in an 1986 story in *Sports Illustrated*. "It's as if it was all mapped out from the start and all that remained to be done was to fill in the blanks one by one. A taste of the bad, then a taste of the good, that's what keeps me going.

"And then I think all the time, Lord, you put me here and gave me success. Are you going to take it away from me one day to see how I react?"

He is preparing for that day, should it come, knowing his place on earth is to do more than just play baseball and be thankful for all that has gone right for him. He is spreading the love of Christ to others, helping children as he needed help.

In Columbus, Georgia, Teresa's hometown, the Davises have opened the Glenn Davis Home for Boys and the Teresa Davis Home for Girls. Davis funds the facilities with the proceeds he receives from appearing at baseball card autograph-signing shows and other off-season public appearances.

Some thirty years later, Glenn Davis has come full circle, fulfilling an early goal—this time with true and loving intentions replacing the phony God-loving pupil he played as an adolescent.

"When my baseball career is over, I want to start a ministry for kids," Davis says. "I think it is my calling. My life has evolved to this. The Lord has put me in a position to give something back to kids who might be as lost as I was. It's the best way I can use the life He has given me. Maybe this is what He intended all along."

GARY
◆ Gaetti ◆
5

A little-known infielder playing in a small media market, Gary Gaetti was an obscure figure in the early days of his professional baseball career. In the fall of 1987, that changed in a matter of weeks. The Minnesota Twins, Gaetti's team for seven seasons, were stunning, upset winners of the World Series.

As the man the Twins called their "banshee leader," Gaetti was at center stage. Delighting in the spotlight, he delivered a profane earful and an irreverent eyeful.

In game situations, Gaetti instigated confrontations with everyone: umpires, opposing players, even teammates. He cussed them all, and himself. When the games ended, Gaetti was never without a can of beer and a puffing cigarette. Four-letter words flowed from his lips, attached to every verb, adjective and noun—as if he didn't know how to converse without them.

There were television crews everywhere filming the scene. Gaetti was their popular subject, even if half the words he uttered had to be edited out for the nightly news.

His teammates watched Gaetti and enjoyed the show. They nicknamed him, "The Rat." Gaetti soon had "The Rat" T-shirts made up with his likeness and his nickname. Everyone concerned agreed: It was the perfect nickname.

When he left the locker room, Gaetti kicked these excesses into an even higher gear. "I knew no bounds," he says. He drank into the wee hours of the night. He chain-smoked between innings of games. In the off-season, there were month-long binges in bars, weekend after weekend away from home.

In the bizarre and sometimes twisted value system in professional sports, Gaetti's behavior was occasionally admired. If he appeared in the locker room before a game sickened by a hangover and still played that day, it was considered a sign of his dedication to the team.

If he started a fight on the field or was thrown out of a game for berating an umpire with profanity, some said it showed Gaetti's marvelous intensity. If he threw his equipment and smashed his bats against the walls of the dugout when he struck out, it showed that he was a "poor loser."

Odd as it may seem, poor losers are often considered good things in baseball. There is a saying, anonymous but oft-quoted: "Show me a good loser and I'll show you a loser."

In this insular atmosphere, Gaetti found many who would encourage his lifestyle. There were those that worried, however. For a good player, a baseball career lasts a dozen years. Some of Gaetti's friends wondered if he could live that long.

"I didn't ever resist temptation," Gaetti says now, looking back on those years, "whether it be physical, or sexual, or a lot of things like that. I used my body a lot. I pretty much lived the way I felt like living. And that meant that I smoked for fifteen years, about two packs a day. All it depended on was how long the game was and how much I had to drink. I was living pretty much full-speed for the devil."

Gaetti has since signed a free agent contract with the California Angels. Sitting outside their locker room, he recalls his past ruefully.

"I was going to be doomed," he says in a soft voice. There is a calm presence to Gaetti now, a quiet demeanor that suggests very little of the belligerent, bellicose Gaetti of old.

Reminded of that Gary Gaetti, he taps his bat lightly at his feet and smiles.

"Jesus enters different people's lives in different ways," he says. "For me, I think I could fool myself for only so long. I knew my life was in need of a big change. I had to change many things. It started with an act of repentance and confession."

Gaetti's conversion came in the summer of 1988. He had recently had knee surgery.

"I was a little disgruntled, upset that I wasn't healthy and contributing the way I wanted to," he says. "I heard a lady talking to a friend about a Bible event that is going to happen but she was told it was going to happen in September of that year. It is the rapture, when we are spirited from the world to meet Jesus.

"I started reading more about this and talking with other Christian ballplayers. It really got me thinking about where I stood in relation to God. It challenged me at the time to think that if Jesus came back in September of that year, where I would be and what I would do? I realized that I needed to change a lot of things in my life or I would be in trouble.

"At that time I really seriously committed my life to following after Jesus Christ. I was rewarded right away. The Bible meant to me what it was supposed to mean to me. I was radically saved in His Word. I now saw what it was He wanted me to see."

Gaetti's conversion was so dramatic, many of his Minnesota teammates did not take it seriously.

"There was a period of adjustment for everyone," he says. "I had to understand. People wondered how it could happen that way and I had to tell them that Jesus works in different ways for all of us. For me, I had to interpret that God was leading by His Holy Spirit one of His chosen people to His Son Jesus Christ to repent.

"It is God's will that every man comes to be saved. I didn't know the Bible before I came to know Jesus but yet, when I did, I knew that His words were life to me and they were something I needed to know.

"Everybody does it differently. God uses people differently and He moves people differently. Another person may read the Bible for twenty years and not really have a relationship with God. But read the Bible, study the Bible, and it's a revelation of who He is."

Though he does not ask or expect any special understanding or treatment, Gaetti has come to realize that his lifestyle as a professional athlete makes special demands on him and his beliefs.

"In some respects, this job, this lifestyle is very hard because of the strongholds of pride and greed and lust and fame and fortune," he says. "It's hard not to succumb to the pressure of failure everyday, the pressure of losing games. Not to succumb to getting angry at the umpires, getting angry at your teammates, getting angry at the other players. To keep it all under control and be a role model.

"You're right out there. People see you doing this and doing that . . . so it's tough. But I like to think that God wants to use me in some way as much as I'm yielded to Him, to affect the lives of people playing the game, people watching the game, and their children.

"In that one respect, I think it's a great platform for God to use somebody, for God to inspire and touch the lives of a group of people that are only interested in sports or baseball or something like that."

And yet, Gaetti knows that he cannot always be comfortable using himself as such an example.

"I'm not saying to look at me. God forbid! Don't look at me, look at Jesus," he says. "See how it all relates in the big picture. If I say something, man, check it out with the Bible, make sure it aligns with what the Bible says.

"You'll know by the fruit if it's of God or not of God. If I go out and commit sin or if I don't keep my anger under control, it's my flesh, it's not God. Don't let something stupid that I do turn you away from God. There is another party involved here. . . . That's the evil one that is the negative force where the battleground is in your mind. That's what lots of people don't realize. What is really happening in the spiritual realm."

Gaetti tried to impart this lesson to his Minnesota teammates, but his new attitude and lifestyle, at least initially, was not welcomed by all.

"To them, I guess I changed drastically," he says. "But I am not docile as a player. Christian athletes all hear the same things about being passive. God still uses qualities like intensity to further His plan. I am a baseball player. That's my job. Jesus says we are supposed to work. But I can't scream and shout at the other team like I used to.

"Still, I find other ways to lead. I lead by example. It's taken time for them to understand that, though."

The message has gotten through. Now in his first season with the California Angels, Gaetti has found that in time, his Christian commitment has been accepted, even by his old teammates with the Twins. Curiously, just as Gaetti's Minnesota contract was expiring in 1990, his faith had ceased to be a source of controversy there.

At one time, Gaetti's conversion was big news, worthy of a six-page feature story in

Sports Illustrated in 1989. These days, Gaetti finds the atmosphere more tranquil. He is part of the clubhouse banter. He jokes easily with his teammates. And he often leads the Sunday chapel sessions that are increasing in attendance throughout the major leagues.

Seated in the Angels dugout before a game at Yankee Stadium in the spring of 1991, Gaetti seems as big a part of the team as ever, constantly calling out encouragement to teammates as they go through their pregame drills.

"I'm still vocal out there," he says. "I just don't use the bad language I used to." And occasionally for inspiration, he sings a hymn or two at his third base position in the infield.

"It's something [Los Angeles Dodgers pitcher] Orel Hershiser did during the World Series in 1988 to relax during games," Gaetti says. "I liked that."

Often, Gaetti will also recite from Philippians 4:13 before an appearance at the plate: "I can do all things through Christ, who strengtheneth me" (KJV).

A former teammate in Minnesota, catcher Brian Harper, says of Gaetti: "He was perhaps too enthusiastic at first. He was so filled with the Spirit. It happens. Now he realizes that, with some people, the best witness you can give them is your life. Your peacefulness and happiness tell others a lot about a life knowing Jesus."

Gaetti acknowledges Harper's suggestion.

"I agree, though it is hard sometimes," he says. "I want everyone to read the Bible so much. I wish everybody would come to know the Lord Jesus. He does too. He'll never force His will upon anybody. You have to yield your will to His. That's how that works.

"People sometimes talk to me like Jesus came to me. Like this was pushed at me. No, that's not it. I could have turned my back on the whole situation. So, if you think that God's going to do it without any help from you, you're wrong. It's not fate. Don't read into it that I'm saying you don't have a choice in the matter, because you do. You can choose to go to heaven and live forever with Jesus and God or you can choose to go to hell. And there is really nothing in between except for this probationary period that we live on earth before the Second Coming.

"In Romans 3:23 God says all have sinned and fallen short of His glory. Now God is either telling the truth or He is lying. And He doesn't lie. But I don't have to sin every day. That's why it's so important to come to know Jesus. If everything that the Bible says is true, and you stand before God on your own, you're doomed, brother. But if you're covered by the blood of Jesus you'll be saved. It's a terrible thing to stand before the living God in your own righteousness knowing that you're doomed.

"I'm still so far from perfect, even with all the Bible words and the leading of the Holy Spirit. I still make major mistakes. I just gotta keep going."

He keeps going, knowing that others are watching him, waiting for him to renege on his commitment. Knowing that he is a visible personality, especially in middle America.

"I am aware that people look at me because I'm a professional athlete," Gaetti says. "But I don't worry so much about being a role model as much as I do about being a witness for Jesus Christ. People watch me now and notice differences in my behavior on the field, but I think they take it wrong.

"In my mind, hopefully the negative parts of that behavior are gone. Before I would use bad language and throw my equipment. I'm still guilty of it—I've done it this year. It's hard. It's not being in control . I think that's where a lot of people get confused about Christians being passive. Because we try to keep the negative emotions in check, a lot of people think that's too passive.

"But the fact is that everybody should try to do that. A lot of players need to work on that, not just the Christian players."

Gaetti sees some of his teammates and believes they could make use of many of the same guidelines he does.

"People ask me how I know how my life should be lived, and I tell them that the Bible tells us so," he says. "What you shouldn't do and just as many things that you should do. And none of us do them all. We're supposed to live this life as though Jesus were coming back tomorrow. If you knew that for a fact, I guarantee you'd change your life.

"Personally, I don't smoke or drink anymore. I don't practice those things as a Christian. I can, but what kind of witness is that being? The Bible says not to do these things and yet you're going to let your will override what the Bible says and go ahead and sin? That's all it would be—it's sin.

"It may not necessarily be a sin that will damage your soul but why let it have a place in your life? It does damage. How am I going to be a witness for kids and tell them not to do drugs, and then go get drunk or smoke a pack of cigarettes? That's not a true witness."

Those who know the old Gary Gaetti are constantly asking him if it was hard to give up his old habits, to give up the smoking and drinking.

"When it came to that, I just asked God," he answers. "I asked God to help me. I used His Word to overcome a lot of those things. The temptation was tough sometimes, but I knew I needed to give them up . . . .

"They make nonalcoholic beer now, and some of it is pretty good. I'll drink a couple of those. It's not intoxicating. That's the whole thing. There is nothing wrong with having a beer or having a glass a wine. There is something wrong with drunkenness.

"It's something that I have to fight all the time. I fight myself. People ask if I'm at peace with myself more than others now, and all I can say is that I'm at peace with God, that's the key. You fight yourself. You have to try to put down the flesh. The flesh tries to rise up all the time.

"I do things I know I shouldn't do and I don't want to do, yet I end up doing them anyway. It's the battleground within your mind. But I am far better than I was in so many ways. I have more patience than I used to, and I don't abuse people like I used to. But telling other people about Jesus Christ and telling them the truth and getting them convicted about where they stand, it can be hard. If they believe in something contrary to the Gospel, then you're not at peace with that person because they don't like to hear that kind of stuff. And yet, I have to love those people because I know God created them."

At the 1989 All-Star Game in Anaheim, California, Gaetti took the opportunity to distribute leaflets to his fellow stars, giving his testimony and a plan for personal salvation. When the national television cameras focused on him during the pregame introductions, he held up his palm, showing a batting glove where he had written: Jesus Is Lord. "I considered that a victory for the Lord," he says. "There might have been somebody out there watching who was living a messed up life and needed help. Maybe he saw the message and it helped him make a decision."

But some in the baseball community resented the gesture.

"There's God in all of us," one All-Star told him. "We don't all have to display it."

"That's kind of a misunderstanding," Gaetti says. "Is there God in all of us? . . . Not necessarily. God created everybody out there but until those people are reborn—born again—then they are children of disobedience.

"Now that doesn't make you a bad person. If you don't know Jesus Christ personally and haven't come to repent, I would just say that you would be classified in the

Bible as a child of disobedience.

"It doesn't mean I don't love you or that I don't like you or that you're a bad guy. But it does classify you in one group or another. That's really how God looks at people. He loves you, but if you stand before Him without the blood of Jesus then you are doomed. That's how it works.

"Jesus knows this. He knows how it is to be a man on this earth. He wouldn't know what it was like to be tempted otherwise. He paid for our sins. He emptied himself.

"That's how we now have the knowledge of the perfect man. We will be like Him someday. You have to keep striving for that. That's the danger of going so far and not going all the way. We're supposed to continue on to that higher calling in Jesus. We try to walk as He did: perfect. That gives us a goal to strive for.

"It's hard; the Lord knows that I stumbled. But He is with you if you get up and try, confess, and repent. And He will reward you if you do. That's why I wish He would come back now and let us all go to heaven. This world doesn't compare to what heaven is like. The Apostle Paul says: 'No eye has seen, no ear has heard, no mind has conceived what God has prepared for those who love Him' " (1 Corinthians 2:9, NIV).

OREL
◆ Hershiser ◆
6

It was April 25, 1990, and Los Angeles Dodgers pitcher Orel Hershiser couldn't imagine what was wrong with his right shoulder. He was standing in the center of a baseball diamond, usually a place of great comfort.

It was from here, on a mound, that his career had taken shape. He took to the rise in the middle of the field to start his games, but soon after he began pitching, it was as if he no longer needed the physical advantage. It was already a mismatch.

Hershiser was not only one of the best players in baseball; in 1988, he had pitched better than anyone in a century of professional baseball seasons.

There was a record 59 scoreless innings pitched, and the Most Valuable Player awards from both the 1988 National League

Championship Series and the subsequent
World Series. That season had begun with
a pitching mound for a stage. By the time
he was through, the world was his stage.

But this feeling on this day in April 1990
was different. His shoulder was stiff. It felt
odd, unstable. And there was pain in his
right arm. A pain that Hershiser could not
place. It was the seventh inning of a game
with the St. Louis Cardinals, but this was
not routine muscle fatigue. No, the realization crept over him as he stood in the
center of his baseball universe: Something
was seriously wrong with his arm.

This is a terrifying moment for a major
league pitcher, especially one of Hershiser's
talent. It is a concert pianist finding numb-
ness in his fingers. A stage actor suddenly
finding his voice tremulous, indistinct.

Hershiser left the game. He was examined by specialists a day later. And two
days after accepting that this pain, this
injury was so very, very different than all
the others suffered in his lengthy professional career, he had major surgery to
reconstruct his right shoulder.

There was shock in the baseball community. Hershiser, while expressing optimism
about his comeback, looked and acted
shocked himself at a press conference just
preceding his surgery.

Nearly a year later, he admitted to the

mix of emotions that enveloped him at the time.

"I admit that I cried about the surgery and I cried about the situation I was put through," he says. "But in time I knew I had a strength of peace. It comes from God. I knew that everything was going to be fine whether I pitched again or whether I didn't.

"Maybe there are some people who saw what happened to me and they're wondering where God was for me. Or they're wondering why He would let something like this happen to a nice person.

"But I don't wonder. They just don't understand. I'm fine. God was in control then and He's in control now. It's the same God in control up there. I learned from Him all the successes of 1988 and I'll learn from Him in this situation no matter what my baseball career becomes from here on."

Hershiser's faith has been rewarded with a comeback story that could be as newsworthy as his spectacular run during the 1988 season. He sat out the remainder of the 1990 season following the California surgery by Dr. Frank Jobe. It was a process that tightened Hershiser's shoulder joint and rebuilt the ligaments and the rim of the shoulder socket.

By spring training in 1991, Hershiser was back at the Dodgers preseason Florida home. He pitched in their minor league system throughout May, approaching his shoulder rehabilitation methodically. His worst setbacks, both physical and mental, were behind him. The days of wondering if he would ever pitch in a professional baseball game again were over.

There was no pain. He made his return to Dodger Stadium May 29, taking to the mound before a cheering, sellout crowd in a start against the Houston Astros.

"It is a dream fulfilled," he says. "I've missed baseball. But I learned that you take something from every life experience."

In his year off from baseball, Hershiser took more than time to rest. "It helped prepare me for my eventual retirement from baseball," he says. "Hopefully, I'll choose that time rather than it being forced on me, but I have my faith, my commitment to Jesus. I'm healthy and I love my family.

"Life will not stop at thirty-two years old if baseball stops for me. There are many other things I can do with my abilities. Life with God is eternal anyway."

Hershiser's confident and composed attitude during the comeback from what many described as career-ending surgery has not surprised any that know him.

This is, after all, the gangly, pale-skinned pitcher who Dodgers manager Tommy

Lasorda watched pitch and then nick-named Bulldog.

"I never really liked that nickname," Hershiser says now, after working his way through the Dodgers minor league teams in a program the Baseball Commissioner's Office terms a thirty-day rehabilitation assignment. "I didn't think I needed a nickname to prove my aggressiveness or anything like that. But I know what Tommy means by it and that's meant to be positive. So it's OK."

You can ask the New York Mets, who were favored to bounce the Dodgers quickly and unceremoniously from the 1988 National League playoffs, about the nick-name. Or even better, question the Oak-land Athletics, prohibitive favorites in the World Series in the same year.

Against the Mets, Hershiser pitched in four games, giving up three runs in 25 innings. Against the Athletics, he won both games he pitched, including the clinch-ing victory. At center stage of not only the sports world, but of a country lured to the story of the Dodgers stunning upset, Hershiser took the final moment of that World Series to kneel in prayer behind the pitching mound. Countless visual and mental images of Orel Hershiser were framed forever.

"It was a brief moment of thanks to the

Lord," Hershiser says. "I knew that it was through Him that all glory is found."

Said Oakland manager Tony LaRussa after his team, considered a budding dynasty, had been eliminated by the Dodgers: "No pitcher I've seen —in such a big setting—has ever seemed as determined and unshakable as Hershiser was."

Not that the Athletics didn't try most of the time-honored baseball tricks to unnerve Hershiser in the World Series.

"The one thing they kept doing was stepping out of the batter's box as I was getting ready to go into my delivery," Hershiser says. "What they didn't realize was that it was only getting me more intensely ready to make the right pitch. They shouldn't have done that."

That's our Bulldog.

And so much for the label that Christian baseball players are less aggressive and competitive than non-Christians.

"I hope we're putting an end to that idea," Hershiser says. "I've said it before: Just because I'm a Christian doesn't mean I'm a wimp. What kind of faith would it be if it made you accept failure? What my faith does is lift me when I have failed. I would betray my faith, betray the world that He has put at my feet for giving myself to Him, if I wasn't completely dedicated to the task of being my best. You do it for

Him. Because it is your job.

"How hypocritical would it be to be a Christian but not to strive to do your best after all He has given you?"

Hershiser accepted Christ as his Savior in 1979, shortly after his first year as a pro in the Dodgers organizational chain. The year began for him in Clinton, Iowa, playing for the Dodgers Class A team. A teammate at Clinton, Butch Wickensheimer, was a Christian and Hershiser says he immediately noticed something different about Butch. It wasn't just his Bible reading; it was his calm, his maturity in a team made up of young adults.

Hershiser says he considered himself "one of the guys," but he couldn't help but be curious and intrigued by Butch Wickensheimer. Minor league baseball is at times similar to a barnstorming tour of small towns, a raucous lifestyle of bus rides and bars. But Orel noticed that Wickensheimer kept to himself.

"He was a nice guy, someone who kept himself ready to play and worked hard," Hershiser says. "He stayed sober."

In his autobiography, *Out of the Blue*, Hershiser wrote of Wickensheimer:

> On the team bus, Butch would try to sit under a light that was working so he could read his Bible. I asked him

what he saw in it. "Everything," he told me. "It's God's gift to man. It tells how much He loves us and how we can know Him."

I thought I knew the Bible. People went to heaven if they were good. Christians were good. Butch had a different idea. He didn't push me, but when I asked, he would explain what the Bible said about heaven. Good people don't go there. Forgiven people do.

"I had much the same reaction most people do at that news," Hershiser says now, more than a decade later. "I was skeptical. I went through this period where I checked everything out. He said everything he told me was in the Bible. It took me a long time, but I looked up the references he was making, and he was right, it was all there.

"I kept playing devil's advocate with Butch. I was curious. And I know I was looking for a way out. I couldn't find one. He was making too much sense.

"But in time, I knew it was my decision. I would have to accept Christianity or reject it. Now I was not a troublemaker. My life wasn't spent in bars or anything. But I knew my life would change radically if I made this step."

Hershiser and Wickensheimer were assigned to the Arizona Instructional League in the fall of 1979 and they shared a room at the Buckaroo Hotel in Scottsdale. Hershiser continued his pestering of Wickensheimer about Christ and the Bible. Hershiser had each of his questions answered, except the one only he himself could truly answer.

One evening, alone in their Scottsdale hotel room, Hershiser was sitting in bed reading the Gideon Bible.

"I cannot explain what it was about that moment," he says. "I certainly did not know that night was going to be any different beforehand. But I got out of bed and prayed. I wanted to say that I knew that I had sinned and that nothing I could do would save me.

"I had been reading the Bible and I knew that Jesus had done that for me. I had to accept Him as my Savior. There was a realization and a willingness. I asked to be a Christian. I accepted Him. And there was an immediate compassion and love that filled me. There was relief. His promises and my understanding of His Word grew from that moment."

In *Out of the Blue*, Hershiser wrote of that night in September 1979:

I figured if God was God, He would understand if I just told Him what was on my mind. I said: "God, I don't know everything about you. I don't think I ever will. But I know I want Christ in my life, and I want to go to heaven. I want to become a Christian. With that, I accept you. Amen."

There were no tears, no lightning, no wind, no visions. I just got back into bed and continued to read the Bible. I knew I had done the right thing. I had stepped from skepticism to belief. God had forgiven me and Christ was in me and the character He had already built into me affected the type of Christian I would become.

God impressed upon me that He would take care of me and love me no matter what. Whether I made the big leagues and became rich and famous and had everything the world has to offer or I failed at baseball, He would be there.

Hershiser says there was a comfort in his new faith that burgeoned spiritually as he enthusiastically studied the Bible. He also met with other Christians. His church going took on new meaning.

"As any Christian will tell you," he says. "It is a change that exhilarates. It fulfills. It makes every experience in your life better."

Curiously, his pitching did not improve

with his attitude and rededicated work habits. At least not initially.

"It was more a matter of inconsistency I think than anything," he says now, looking back at the twenty-two-year-old Orel Leonard Hershiser IV who compiled a 5-9 record at San Antonio in 1980. "It's pretty typical of a minor league pitcher still learning to pitch."

San Antonio brought Hershiser far more than a second year of professional baseball, though. Attending church during that summer in Texas, Hershiser put on his prayer list a request to meet a Christian woman who shared his values and morals.

"Three days later, I met Jamie at a party," he says. "I didn't remember my prayer request at the time. Even after she told me she was a Christian. But there was a link that seemed right from the beginning."

Jamie Byars and Hershiser were engaged six weeks later, and married the following spring, in 1981.

"The story always sounds like we didn't know what we were doing and it might have seemed so soon," Hershiser says. "But all I can say is that there's no doubting now that we were right for each other. Jamie has been with me for everything. She shares every frustration and every victory."

There is, of course, the semifamous story

of Hershiser wanting to practice a new kink in his delivery one evening in their home during the mid-1980s. Only Jamie was around to catch his pitches. While she had tried to help him before, she still couldn't handle a 90 mile-an-hour fastball—not in baseball form, at least.

So Orel made his throws, and, with Jamie's help, the duo examined his pitching form as he hurled rolled up socks toward her.

As *Sports Illustrated* wrote at the conclusion of this oft-quoted story: "It was argyles, low and away."

When Orel was called up for his first full season with the Dodgers in 1984, it was sinkers low and away. And success and fame to follow.

In 1984, as both a reliever and starting pitcher, Hershiser had an 11-8 record with a 2.66 earned-run average. The following season, used almost exclusively as a starter, he hit stride. His 19-3 record gave him the best winning percentage in the National League and his ERA of 2.03 was unheard of for a starting pitcher in the new "live ball" era.

A nation of sports writers flocked to the Los Angeles locker room to find out who the skinny right-hander with the unusual name and stunning record of victories was.

"It caught me by surprise," Hershiser

says. "The attention I mean. But I enjoyed it. I did remind myself that I had to be sure to dedicate myself all that much more to preparing to pitch. I refused to be distracted."

Still, as often happens for pitchers, there were circumstances beyond his control. The next two years the Dodgers were a losing team, with identical 30-89 season records. Not surprisingly, for Hershiser those two seasons brought a combined 30-30 record. He pitched well and his ERA remained low. In 1987, he proved his reliability to his team by leading the league in innings pitched.

But a pitcher likes to win his games, and your teammates' offensive difficulties are not considered an acceptable excuse for lost games. Hershiser took it as another of life's lessons.

"It was frustrating at times, but I never felt burdened," he says. "I don't like failure but I'll deal with it. It used to be so much harder. I let it eat at me. But Jesus helped me so much. My faith is very personal and I use it to guide me.

"If I lose, I don't like it. But I get strength from knowing that it is insignificant in relation to others things. God still loves me. My wife and family still love me. That's the big thing. The world will hardly come to an end because I lose a baseball game."

In 1988, Orel Hershiser turned the baseball world on end because he hardly lost a baseball game. His season record was 23-8, but that does not adequately describe how he concluded the year unscored upon for 59 innings. It was a streak that extended Don Drysdale's old record by an inning. Drysdale's mark, set in the 1960s when pitching dominated the game, had been filed in the category of unbreakable. It was thought of as an aberration, a great accomplishment attained when the balance between pitcher and hitter was skewed unfairly toward the man throwing the baseball.

Since then, baseball had altered several rules—and most likely increased the liveliness of the ball itself—to bring the hitters even again. All over major league baseball hitting statistics were up.

Everywhere, except in games that Hershiser pitched. He led the big leagues in victories. The National League in innings pitched. His ERA was an unheard of number from the past, 2.26.

He was not only a good pitcher, but reporters found him good copy. He smiled and made jokes. He told stories. And he had a way of talking about his Christian faith that made it into the stories of mainstream journalism, a somewhat rare accomplishment.

"There is no underestimating what Orel did for the Christian athlete in 1983," New York Mets pitcher Tim Burke says. "The understanding that we are every-day people with dreams and hopes and desires to win came through so obviously. He was such a good pitcher and likable guy. I know of dozens of Christian baseball players who wrote or personally thanked Orel for that season. It was a big step toward our acceptance."

When the World Series was over, what one could call Hershiser's "Good Will Tour" continued in a big way. He appeared as a guest on "The Tonight Show." Host Johnny Carson asked Hershiser about the close-ups the network television cameras had made of him during the World Series as he sat in the Dodgers dugout.

Hershiser explained, as he had before, that he was singing hymns to relax himself. Carson urged him to sing on the show. Then Carson enlisted the audience's help in coaxing Hershiser to sing.

At first Orel resisted, but then he sang what he called a favorite:

> Praise God from whom all blessings flow.
> Praise Him all creatures here below.
> Praise Him above ye heavenly host.
> Praise Father, Son, and Holy Ghost.

Since his shoulder surgery, there have been tougher times for his baseball career than that moment on late-night television. The network cameras have not caught Hershiser singing as he labored through countless hours to break down the scar tissue in his shoulder. Through the hours to strengthen the muscles in his right arm. Through the frustrations of not being able to throw the ball as hard and as accurately as before, and through the practice it took to regain that velocity and control.

The spotlight has not been there for those struggles. Reporters have not accompanied him through every stage. Baseball fans certainly have not lost their respect nor their good intentions for Hershiser, but their attention has been focused elsewhere.

But Orel Hershiser says he has not worked alone. And he will not come back to baseball alone.

"God never abandons you," he says. "Christianity is called a spiritual walk. It's not a run and it's not a jog. It's a walk you do from day to day and that makes you stable. When you walk, you will remain stable, with one foot on the ground. That foot is based in what you believe. It's your faith. When you're running, you're unstable. Something can come along and bump you, and knock you offstride. If you approach your life and your career that way—a day-to-day walk with your faith— you will stay stable. You can be ready for changes."

The sudden loss of his pitching ability shocked but did not change Orel Hershiser.

"My relationship and my faith in God made all the difference in how I could handle the tougher times," he says, smiling. "I know there have been times in the last year that people have said: 'It doesn't look like Orel is going to make it back.' But it doesn't bother me.

"They don't know how hard I work, how hard my faith motivates me to do my best. And then I can say: 'Lord, wherever or whatever you want for me, that's where I'll go or what I'll do.'

"You really have to realize it's in the Lord's hands. And there's no place that I could feel more comfortable."

STEVE
◆ Howe ◆
7

Baseball, every sports fan should know by
now, keeps very good records. The people
who run and record the game keep track of
everything. And not just statistics. A
player's personal biography can be very
personal.

Tucked away in the files of the Baseball
Commissioner's Office there is a biography
of pitcher Steve Howe that is three times as
thick with his missteps, near-arrests, and
utter embarrassments than with his bril-
liant, if brief baseball successes.

Howe is just thirty-three years old, but
he has been in the spotlight for twelve
years. And the glare always seems to have
caught him in a place he does not belong,
doing something that wrongs himself and
those around him. The Howe file, kept so
fastidiously by the baseball community, is

an astounding litany of self-destruction.

Of course, it details Howe's All-American status as a pitcher at the University of Michigan. It lists his honors as the National League's Rookie of the Year in 1980. It notes that he saved the final game of the 1981 World Series as the Los Angeles Dodgers defeated their old rivals, the New York Yankees. And he was an All-Star in 1982.

On-the-field data all but end there, in the summer of 1982. Read the rest, and wonder how Steve Howe is still alive:

—November 1982: spent five weeks in an Arizona drug rehabilitation center for cocaine abuse. Dismissed to resume playing with the Dodgers, Howe was back at a southern California rehab center in May 1983.

—Reinstated by the Dodgers in June, he was suspended from the team again when he showed up three hours late for a game in July. Reinstated two days later, Howe was suspended again when he failed to come to the ballpark for a game September 24.

—After sitting out the 1984 major league season because of a suspension imposed by the Baseball Commissioner's Office, Howe pitched in an Arizona instructional league and rejoined the Dodgers in early 1985.

—On June 23, 1985, Steve Howe did not arrive for a game until the seventh inning.

Six days later, he did not show at a charity dinner for which he was chairman. He also missed the Dodgers game the next day.

—The Dodgers finally released Howe later in 1985. He was picked up by the Minnesota Twins. Howe was pitching with some success for the Twins when, on September 12, they granted him permission to miss a team flight to Cleveland so he could appear on television's "Nightline" program. Howe not only missed the program appearance, but he also did not make it to Cleveland. He missed five consecutive Twins games before contacting Minnesota officials and admitting to a relapse of his cocaine abuse.

—In 1986, released by the Twins, Howe pitched in the minor leagues at San Jose, California. Tested by the Baseball Commissioner's Office, he twice showed positive for drugs.

—By 1987, Howe was pitching for Tabasco of the Mexican League. The Texas Rangers signed him late in the 1987 season, and he pitched well. In the off-season, he failed another test related to his after-care program. The Rangers released him.

And that's not the half of it. Howe's wife of twelve years could tell you worse stories.

"He was so very sick. I mean, what he wouldn't do to get the drugs," Cindy Howe says. "I tell you, you wouldn't believe it."

He would leave the house to rent a videotape or to go to the bank and not return for three days. He so depleted their bank account that, despite a six-figure salary from Steve, the family was forced to sell their modest home to keep from defaulting on their mortgage. Once, Cindy Howe, at wit's end, contacted the police to have one of Steve's drug buddies arrested for dealing.

"There were times he came home that I felt sure I was watching him die," she says.

In his darkest thoughts, Howe wondered if maybe it wouldn't be better if he did.

"What I really wanted to do was disappear from the earth," Howe says now. "I contemplated disappearing for my family's good. I didn't know how to do it, to make it work in a way that didn't cause more trouble. But I felt like I should disappear. I was torn because I wanted to stay and watch my kids grow up, but I didn't want my kids going to school and having to hear the other kids say, 'So how's your father the drug addict?'

"It was my lowest point. I just felt I had lost my whole vision, all my hope. Everything was slipping away. I loved my family, and yet I didn't feel worthy to stay."

Howe speaks now from the comfortable digs of the New York Yankees princely players' clubhouse. It is May 1991, and he says he has been clean for thirty-one months. He has been tested thrice weekly for the last year of that period as a way of proving his drug-free lifestyle.

Howe has returned to the major leagues, pitching fastballs and hard-breaking sliders with incredible velocity for a man his age. He is, again, a professional baseball player of value. On May 19, he earned the victory for the Yankees against the Seattle Mariners, his first win since 1987. In the moments following that game, Howe smiled so hard it seemed his face would crack.

Asked to explain his comeback, exacted this time against the longest odds yet, he says: "It's so simple, that I know you wouldn't believe me. How did this all happen? I asked Jesus to help me. I know people don't believe me. I used to be one of those people. I didn't believe it either. It's OK. The Lord is patient."

Hours before the game on that May day, Howe treated his left arm—twice surgically repaired—to a whirlpool bath. Asked to recall his strife-ridden path, Howe nods toward the bubbling water in the stainless steel tub.

"I was drowning just as if I had stuck my head under this water and kept it there for ten years," he says. "I was killing myself. I didn't like who I was. I didn't like where I came from. I didn't like where I felt I was going. I felt I was weak. I felt I couldn't shake this thing. I felt I had made nothing

but bad choices. I just didn't like myself.
Booze wasn't really my deal; my problem
was cocaine. It was the drug of my choice.
It was supposedly what worked for me,
what was supposedly going to take away
the bad feelings. I sat there like a veg-
etable.

"I did whatever was there. Any amount
of grams. I could never tell you what I
spent on drugs back then. But it certainly
cost me eight to ten million in salary in
baseball. I know that people who knew
that Steve Howe probably think of me now
and don't believe that I was able to change
my life. They say that I should be angry for
all the time I wasted. Sure, I can look back
at my life and wonder why I wasted so
much time.

"But we all find the Lord's message differently. I'm not God, so I don't know why
it worked this way, but I guess these things
had to happen before I knew it was my
time to choose His way. I certainly had
exhausted every other avenue. I was a lost
cause. But, of course, you never really are.
All you have to do is surrender to Jesus. I
just didn't know that yet."

Howe's odyssey of nonstop drug use took
its life-saving turn in January 1989, in
Whitefish, Montana, where he and his
family had settled after his release by the
Texas Rangers. He had pitched only spo-

radically for minor league teams in 1988. He had another serious arm injury that needed surgery. And he was admitted to another drug treatment center, his eighth in the previous five years.

He left the center late in 1988. It was a time of absolute turning points. Cindy Howe had let her husband know that this time, without reprieve, another relapse meant that she would be leaving—with their daughter, Chelsi, and son, Brian.

The couple's local pastor, Al Barone, greeted Howe on his return to Whitefish. He had a deal. "He told me that all I had to do was surrender to Jesus," Howe says. "And I said, 'That's it?' I figured this would be easy. I was always figuring that I had every gimmick figured out. For years, I had been calling myself a Christian. I had been baptized in 1982, but I was still fence jumping so to speak. I'd jump on the fun side, and then come back over and ask for forgiveness. Ask God to get me out of this jam that I was in. I did that for six years.

"The fact is, I had tried everything in my power to get off drugs. I was getting nowhere. As I said, I had a head knowledge of this God, but part of me I think was really scared of Him. Because what if I tried God and that didn't work? Then what did I have?

"Of course from what I know now, Jesus

doesn't let us down. Those are His promises, and they all are fulfilled. But in late 1988 and early 1989, I was so very skeptical. A friend, Harold Peterson, and Al Barone just kept telling me, 'Steve, all you've got to do is surrender.'

"I really couldn't believe it. It was the hardest thing for me. I just couldn't grasp that it could be that easy. Finally, I said: 'OK, teach me.' "

Howe says he was not prepared for what he heard next.

"They said that first I had to do a few things to make my commitment total," he recalls. "I asked them what they were. They said that I had to take a full year off from baseball. I looked at them and stood up and yelled, 'What!'

"But they knew something that I didn't. That as long as I had baseball, which had been my god, I wasn't going to give everything I had to Jesus. That's what I needed to do, turn everything over to Him. I looked around at my life, I thought about how I was on the verge of disappearing, and I knew what I had to do."

Steve Howe turned his life over to God completely. He painted the church in Whitefish. He drove people without the use of a car to their doctor's appointments. He did favors for anyone who needed the help.

"I became a servant of the church," Howe says. "For a year, I did whatever was needed. I started doing things for other people and it took me away from my so-called problems. All of a sudden, I didn't have any problems. I did have all the same worries as anyone else. I worried for my family. But I was taken care of. God's works in my life were enormous. I had to go through a lot of circumstances that were very painful to see them. If I would have known God's character, I wouldn't have had to go through what I had to go through. But that is the way He guides. You must come to Him.

"Eventually, I gave all things to Him. Then, there were so many things provided me, prayers met, financially and otherwise. I was told to believe in Him and He would take care of me, and that's what happened. The ways that it happened, I considered coincidences early in my walk. But now I just believe. If I pray, I don't even worry. I just know it will work out. It's like tithing. I give Him 10 percent of everything I make. I get back fifty times more than I could ever give. These are things I had to learn.

"Look at my baseball career. I had given up my career. I gave it to the Lord. Next thing I knew, in two years He gave it back."

Still, there were trying moments. In early 1989, especially, the temptations were enormous.

"There was a night, a moment that signaled the biggest turnaround for me," Howe says. "But it was terrifying. I had been to a meeting the evening before, and the subject was blackouts—the times when you're drunk or on drugs and you're walking around doing things that you're not even conscious of."

Steve came home from the meeting and went to bed. But he could not sleep. He got up and went downstairs to the dining room.

"I had remembered that in a blackout months before, I had hid a bag of cocaine," he says. "Now, I believe Satan revealed to me where that cocaine was because I certainly had not remembered before this. So I got it, and I felt like a caged animal. That stuff is so powerful. The draw is immense.

"But for the first time in my life, I flushed it down the toilet. I had a choice to make. Even I couldn't believe it the next day. I flushed about a thousand dollars of the stuff down the toilet. That was it. That was the moment."

Steve's return to the major leagues was a long process still. He had to pitch for a few minor league teams, and there was a serious injury to his left arm. There were complications in the surgery correcting the problem. A blood clot in Howe's lung nearly killed him.

After a month in a California hospital, the Howes returned to Whitefish for the winter of 1990-91 without a baseball contract. Steve's agent, Dick Moss, called every big league team. Only the Yankees would even listen.

Steve got on the phone to Yankees general manager Gene Michael. "Please give me a chance," he said.

Says Michael: "If he were my son, I'd want someone to give him a chance."

So the Yankees watched Steve Howe pitch in spring training and offered him a contract.

"Cindy and I cried," Howe says. "Another promise fulfilled by the Lord. I wish I had seen His way sooner. But I realize that Jesus is patient. Jesus grieves when He sees that we are going to injure ourselves. But He has to be patient because He must wait. We must choose our path. He gives us a choice.

"We can choose our way or His way. We can read His Word, but we must accept it. People for the most part are skeptical because throughout life we get burned. When I finally wised up, everything changed for the better."

That includes Howe's on-the-field

performance.

"It's amazing because now I can play so relaxed and I can really concentrate," he says. "Because I am at peace. I have Him in my life. My family has been restored. I can walk with my head high. Be humble. Be proud. I didn't feel that I had to do it all myself anymore. I'm out there and I know I am a lucky man. And I am grateful."

Steve's story became a favorite topic for sports writers across the nation in the spring of 1991. He says he enjoyed explaining how his life was saved, so long as he was not expected to bemoan his many years of personal failure.

"I don't want people to judge me for the things I did wrong in the past," he says. "It's just the way things were going to happen for me, unfortunately. Sure, part of me might want to think, 'Boy, what a waste.' But it was going to take me a long time to find the way, period. I had no idea what I was all about. I was a very angry young man. Angry about certain circumstances in my life that were uncomfortable to me.

"Everyone always said about me, 'Oh, he's such a likable person. He's seemingly intelligent.' And they couldn't understand how I could be making such destructive choices. It's true that the Lord doesn't want any of us to suffer. But I just couldn't make good choices. Now I try to make better choices. What I try to do is carry Jesus with me. When I have to make a choice or decision, I ask myself what would I do if Jesus were sitting here with me.

"I was just talking to my wife the other day about this. I still smoke. It's one of my vices. I told her I just couldn't picture myself sitting there smoking a cigarette with Jesus. It's a visual image I use. I want to get my smoking over with. I give up the right to tell my children not to smoke if I smoke. So I'm going to stop. I know He can help me when the time is right. Look what He did for my terrible drug addiction. It's been two and one-half years now and I don't have the desire to do drugs since I turned my life over to Him. At one time, my mind was totally occupied with obtaining and using drugs."

Still, anyone with a history of public drug use as lengthy as Steve Howe's will be met with disbelief about his new, clean habits.

"I know I am not accepted at times," he says. "The Bible says that they will persecute you. People say to me: 'Oh, you're into religion now.'

"And I tell them that I'm not into religion. I have a personal relationship with God. Big difference. The Bible says, 'Great peace have they who love [God's] law and nothing can make them stumble' (Psalm 119:165, NIV). That can't get any more final than that. That's the promise. But it also has the prerequisite that you have to follow the Lord. God's Word, not man's. That's what we must do."

Though his baseball career has bloomed anew, Howe is already looking to the future when his fastball no longer cruises past home plate in excess of 90 miles an hour.

"I want to help kids." he says. "I don't know what kind of ministry I'll have, but my wife and I are excited about the future. I already do a lot of counseling and educating at alcoholism and drug centers and I use Christian principles there. It's what I've learned. I could have gone to 500 treatment centers where they would have told me how messed up I was. But Jesus has already told me what a rotten dude I am . . . the important message that follows that is that the Bible also says, 'Therefore, there is no condemnation for those who are in Christ Jesus' (Romans 8:1, NIV). We are all forgiven if we ask for His forgiveness. I believe wholeheartedly that only a spiritual experience with God can fill the inner man. We need it.

"I know I needed it. I was on a path that was only going to get me killed. Now I walk a path that can only take me to eternal salvation. Can the right choice be any more obvious than that?"

HOWARD
◆ Johnson ◆
8

Howard Johnson has played baseball virtually all his life. He's been paid to play it since he was nineteen.

"It sounds obvious, but you're always told it's a game, a place to have fun," he says. "And yet, I look around and see guys on a roller coaster. Half the time, they're not enjoying the game at all.

"To them, baseball is a game spent living on the edge. Tension is a constant part of life for so many players. If they go into a slump, their whole personality changes. They're depressed and down. It makes it so hard. It is the same way if they're going good. They're flying high.

"There is so much pressure living that way. Imagine having your whole personality tied to hitting or catching a ball."

Johnson, who came to the New York

Mets in 1985 after two seasons with the
Detroit Tigers, knows the life. He lived it.
In his case, through more ups than downs.
But he wasn't immune when an injury to
his right shoulder brought surgery in Oc-
tober 1988, then uncertainty about his
career, and ultimately doubt about everything in his future.

Come the spring of 1989, Johnson, known
as "HoJo" to one and all in the baseball
community, was so obsessed with the
health of his repaired, yet not fully recovered, shoulder, that he often wandered the
Mets clubhouse with a far-off, confused
expression on his face. His teammates
worried for him. They knew how failure
troubled any major league player, perhaps
especially Howard Johnson.

After all, wasn't Johnson the one, who,
during a slump in the middle of the 1988
season, lugged his bats to his bed at home
and slept with them for good luck?

That was HoJo.

Reporters covering the team that spring
at first felt obligated to question Johnson
about the shoulder, but as Johnson made
more throwing errors in exhibition games,
most avoided his locker. The concern and
distress he felt was obvious. An infielder
with an inaccurate arm, one caused by a
serious injury, is soon an infielder without
a job.

In time, Johnson's shoulder problems ceased. His throwing became reliable again. In fact, offensively, he had a career-high season in 1989, batting .287, hitting 36 home runs, and driving in 101 runs. But Johnson remembers the heights of his depression. The depths of his anguish.

"I'm glad I don't have to live through it again," he says. "I'm glad I don't have to live that way at all—the ballplayer's way of life, always on the edge. Christ helped me get off that edge. You know, pressure and anxiety plague our society. And the Lord wants us to put those things upon Him. So now, if I strike out or make an error, or if I hit a home run, my attitude is the same. I'm out there having fun. The game itself becomes pressure-free, and you play better and more consistently that way."

In the fall of 1990, Johnson gave his life to Christ, and for the 1991 baseball season he says he has not only found renewed success on the field, but he has embraced its joys with a new vigor as well.

"It's amazing how the game becomes more fun and how you play better when you take the field pressure-free," he says. "I don't waste time worrying about things so when I'm out on the field my intensity level has actually picked up. People are always watching Christian athletes closely, trying to see if there is some way they will be less involved, but I love the game more than ever. I pursue baseball success with more energy than ever. I'm out there having fun, I want to succeed, and winning is more fun than losing."

Johnson's situation is more taxing than most in major league baseball. The New York Mets are a team loaded with talent, but burdened by the demands of an immense fan base that accepts nothing less than championships. Each game is performed under the scrutiny of dozens of reporters representing outlets from the largest media center in the world.

Johnson knew this all too well from his previous seasons with the Mets. But in 1991, more attention has been focused on him than ever. Johnson, after all, is the team's last remaining true power hitter with the departures of Darryl Strawberry, Gary Carter, Kevin Mitchell, and Keith Hernandez in the last few years. He is also in the middle of the debate over which of the Mets' six infielders should start in the four available spots. And who is best suited to play where? Is Johnson a third baseman? Or a shortstop?

Pressure? Its address is New York's Shea Stadium.

Interesting that Johnson came to the Mets because his former manager in

Detroit, Sparky Anderson, did not think he could perform adequately in pressure situations. Anderson wondered if Johnson lacked the aggressiveness for the clutch situation.

In the intensity of the 1984 American League Championship Series and World Series, for example, Anderson trusted Johnson with only one at-bat in the eight games played. This after Johnson had made 402 plate appearances and played in 116 of 166 regular season games for Anderson in 1984. With Anderson's encouragement, the Detroit front office traded Johnson to the Mets before the beginning of the 1985 season.

The Mets learned that Anderson's assessment could not have been farther off base. In his seven seasons with the Mets, Johnson has hit more home runs from the seventh inning on—when games are likely to be decided and extra base hits are more prized—than any other Met. More than Strawberry. More than Carter or Hernandez.

He helped lead the Mets to their come-from-behind victories in the National League Championship Series and the World Series in 1986. And in 1987, he joined the exclusive 30-30 club by stealing 32 bases and hitting 36 homers in the same season.

Then in 1989, he became just the second player in major league history to have a 30-30 season twice. Along the way, he hit crucial, pressure home runs that his teammates recalled months later as turning points of the title-winning seasons in 1986 and 1988.

There was his game-tying, two-run, ninth-inning home run off Todd Worrell in St. Louis early in the 1986 season. While the Mets would later run away from the Cardinals in winning the division title, several Mets looking back on 1986 in the off-season said Johnson's clutch hit in that game gave them the confidence they needed early on in their challenge to the defending champs from St. Louis.

In 1988, Johnson did much the same in Pittsburgh, cracking a two-out, two-run, ninth-inning homer off Pirates bullpen ace Jim Gott to win a July game. The two teams were close in the standings at that point of the season. The victory in that game, however, set the Mets off on a tear that saw them eliminate Pittsburgh from the race in early September.

"It's hard not to feel the pressure," Johnson says of those heroics. "And I enjoyed being able to do well when it was needed for the team. But I have to say that now I am even better prepared for it. God has helped me see ways through the distractions the pressure can offer. I'm a baseball player; that's what God has given me the talent to do. It's what He wants me to do. And so I'm out there to work.

"All He asks is that I be the best player I can be. So I make sure I am concentrating. I make sure I am focused and that I have prepared with practice and have prepared for the game mentally. So long as I know that I'm trying my best, I can just play. What I do will not change my status with God. It won't be the end all for the truly important things in my life.

"That's not to say that I just throw my glove out there. The glove is not going to catch the ball for me. I don't stand at home plate and wait for the bat to hit the ball, either. I tried to succeed and win. But I'm not living on the edge, with each at-bat deciding my mood and my love for the game. It's what I do. It's the game I love."

The game has loved him back, with awards and accolades by the bushelful. He has been an All-Star, the National League's player of the month four times. During one game in Chicago's Wrigley Field in September 1988, he had five hits in five plate appearances with five RBIs. Three times, he has hit two home runs in one game.

Johnson has not only helped his team in the obvious ways; he is a popular, respected player. A quiet leader. Soft-spo-

ken, Johnson is known in the Mets clubhouse for his personal, low-profile chats
with younger players. One such player,
Kevin Miller, specifically remembers Johnson cheering him up and offering guidance
with a long talk during the 1990 season.

Miller, in his first full season as a major
leaguer, had begun the year as the Mets
everyday center fielder. After only a few
weeks, he was down to playing just every
other day. And within two months, he was
a reserve, playing a utility role.

"I was really down, I felt like I was never
going to get another chance," Miller says.
"HoJo just took me aside. He was very
supportive. He told me how much more of
my career there was ahead of me. He told
me stories about himself and about other
players who had gone through what I had.
He just talked to me like you would a
friend. And that's what he is, a friend. He
tries to be a friend to everyone."

"There's no effort in trying to help someone who is down," Johnson says. "There's
no effort in most of the good things you can
do in your life."

In the 1991 season, one of those things
for Howard has been to try to set an example for others.

"I think we as baseball players are in a
good position to do that," he says. "God
made me a ballplayer not a preacher, but I

think He'd want me to spread the Gospel when I'm asked. I can get the Gospel out to my teammates and to all the thousands of people who follow our team. I use my success or my failure, and I let it be a witness to Jesus Christ.

"I asked Christ into my life in the fall after the 1990 season. And when I went to spring training in 1991 I was determined not to compromise my faith. I professed it to my teammates and the media, and, through them, the fans. I wanted them to know that I was a different person. I wanted them to see what it had done for me. That I would work harder.

"I wanted people to ask me about it. I wanted to tell them."

Johnson was raised a Baptist in Florida. He attended church. He considered himself a Christian.

"I always thought of myself as a good person," he says. "I wanted to do what was right. I didn't drink or smoke. I stayed out of trouble. In fact, for a while I dated a preacher's daughter, so I thought I had first-hand experience as far as what a Christian lifestyle was all about.

"But now looking back, I realize that I didn't completely understand what it was all about. I guess that's common. When people accept Christ, they don't realize what condition they were in before. Years later, while I still thought of myself as a good family man, my wife, Kim, started going to a local church on Long Island where we live now. We got to talk to people there who influenced us about Christ and what He had done for all of us. We started reading the Bible and talking to people at church meetings who could answer the questions we had from our readings.

"In a short time, I came to the realization that Christ really never was number one in my life. He wasn't what I lived for at all. For all practical purposes, I pushed God aside. I was living for me. I didn't want to relinquish control.

"There wasn't any disaster in my life or anything. I had a beautiful family and two nice kids with another on the way. But I just knew and felt that I was not being honest with myself. I had not given myself to Christ. I thought of myself as a Christian, but if I looked at my life, there really was no evidence of that."

In the latter part of 1990, there followed for Howard Johnson a period of soul-searching. "There was a lot of prayer and a lot of Bible reading," he says. "And I came to realize that I wanted to give my life to Christ. My wife and I were watching an evangelical videotape. It was Halloween night, 1990. And I decided that evening to give my life to the Lord.

"I wasn't doing it so God would bless me in other areas, like my career or my life or my family. I did it because it was the right thing to do and it gave me the opportunity to thank God for all that He has done for me."

Johnson felt the change in his life immediately.

"I realized that I had been living with an attitude of 'What happened to Howard Johnson?' every day of my life. It's so much harder if you're worried about how you're faring every day. Instead of that being what drove me each day, the focus of my life became being a Christian, having compassion and love for others, and being a good witness to Him and to a Christian lifestyle. I was no longer putting me first, but putting the Lord first.

"There were certain things I had to give up. My attitude toward people changed. I saw the world through different eyes. I had to study the Bible and pray. I went through a change. You look at things from a different perspective.

"We are so conditioned—especially professional athletes—to think that everything we do is what is most important. Your personal well-being is what comes first in your thoughts. That might seem OK, but when that truly becomes your reason for living, you find that eventually those things wear out and then you're left with nothing.

"I enjoy playing ball, but I found that I could be a better person and a better player by putting the Lord first."

Johnson's conversion occurred at about the same time that two teammates from the 1990 Mets were becoming Christians: Darryl Strawberry and Tim Teufel. Strawberry's commitment to Christ has brought an unusual comparison for Johnson.

"Darryl signed a free agent contract with the Los Angeles Dodgers during the off-season, so we were no longer teammates. But similar things happened to us in the same time period and we were mentioned together since we were former teammates," he says. "But really, I was the opposite of Darryl. He had such bad problems with alcohol. I didn't. But I thought there was a lesson in that, too. There are different ways to get the message."

In Teufel, now with the San Diego Padres, Johnson found a friend, a person with whom he could study the Bible, concentrating on passages that are especially meaningful to those who have recently accepted Christ into their lives.

One of the things Teufel and Johnson have discussed is consistency.

"We both think it's important that we

are consistent in our witness," Johnson says. "People say it is easier for the Christian ballplayer to be accepted now, and it is in some ways. But in other ways, it's tougher because there are players who have declared themselves Christians who have not been consistent in their walk. Some of their attitudes aren't consistent. And the media and their teammates pick up on that immediately. It's noticed immediately.

"Tim and I both wondered how our respective teammates would react to us. But I trusted that if I showed I was sincere in my beliefs, they would understand. And they have. Still, there's a lot we can do as professional baseball players. I know He wants me to help educate people about Christians and the peace we have with our lives. We can be examples. And as someone who recently became a Christian, I know people are watching me. I want them to see that it would only make me work harder.

"It's not something that you can really explain to some people, that a conversion to Christianity will only make you work harder. But I know people were watching me, to see if I changed my game in some sort of passive way. It was important to me that I show them that would not happen. I had to convince them by my actions. You can fill a room up with words about God, but you must prove it with your actions."

At home, as in his career, Johnson has also found more calm, a greater enjoyment.

"I always enjoyed my family, but I appreciate them more than ever," he says. "It's a Christian atmosphere in all the ways we want it to be. My wife and I are concerned with being a good example to our kids [seven-year-old Shannon Leigh and four-year-old Glenn] and to our friends. We never were people that thought hanging around in bars was a good time, but even less so now. At home, we raise our kids to know that there should be a prayer to thank God before each meal. And my daughter attends a Christian school.

"Our lifestyles have to be consistent with our walk, too. People on the outside sometimes depict a Christian lifestyle as being a hard and strict path to follow. As if it's a big list of do's and don'ts.

"That's not it at all, and I only wish they knew that. You don't want to do so many things, not because of a list of requirements, but because you know it's wrong and you just don't want to. What results is that, day-to-day, it really is a more peaceful, easy existence."

MARK
◆ Langston ◆
9

Baseball success has put Mark Langston in the spotlight nearly all his life. He would accept the focus, if only he could redirect it.

"People ask me if a prominent baseball player can set an example of how to live," Langston says. "I tell them that I'm not a very good example alone. No way. I'm a human being and I mess up like anyone else. I know that people look at baseball players in different ways, but I'm not encouraging that.

"What I do tell them is that I'm a mirror and I reflect the Lord's love. It's not me you see leading this life, it's Him. I'm not someone to look up to. When people put expectations on other people in this world, there's always a letdown somewhere. That's not what being a Christian or being on this earth is supposed to be about.

"It's not me that you look at when you examine the inner peace and joy a Christian has, it's what the Lord has done for me. What He has done in me."

It's a message Langston had to learn early and it is one he had to repeat over and over in his brief, yet high-profile, baseball career.

Expectations, the pressure they create, and the pull and tug on a young man labeled with one of the truly dangerous words in sports—"potential"—have sent the thirty-year-old Langston through an emotional roller coaster.

Langston has been given much but he admits that without Christ in his life, his athletic talents would have only led him into situations too burdensome for him to handle.

"I have to be thankful that the Lord does not put us in situations we cannot handle," he says. "But I still know that had I not accepted Christ into my life in 1981, I don't know how I would have gotten through some of the years that followed.

"The 1990 season was a far tougher year than I could have ever imagined having in my life. I really don't know how I would have gotten through it if I wasn't a Christian.

"It was a year when I've leaned on the Lord. And He picked me up every time."

In every way, the 1990 baseball season should have been Mark Langston's happiest personally and finest professionally. He was, after all, coming home to southern California to play for the California Angels. He had signed a record-setting, five-year, $15 million free agent contract to play for a rising team after six seasons pitching for the struggling Seattle Mariners.

Born in San Diego, raised in Santa Clara, and a college baseball star at San Jose State, Mark Langston seemed the embodiment of the California golden boy. Blond hair, blue eyes, with a golden left arm that delivered a baseball to home plate in excess of 95 miles an hour, Langston had it all.

"Even my favorite band is from California, the Beach Boys," he says. "I figured I'd go see them whenever I wanted."

And music is no small interest for Langston. He plays the drums and piano and takes a guitar with him on road trips.

But at the start, Langston hit nothing but wrong notes for the Angels. His early performances were a struggle.

The big contract only intensified the scrutiny on Langston's pitching troubles. In the previous three seasons, he had compiled a 50-38 record, impressive by anyone's standards, but if there were figures Angels fans saw when they looked at Langston in the course of the 1990 season, they were larger-than-life dollar signs.

They booed him off the mound several times at Anaheim Stadium when the opponent's bat boomed louder than the thump of Langston's noted fastball in the leather of the catcher's mitt. Langston pressed to improve, to help his teammates—many of whom were also having poor seasons—and to show the hometown fans the kind of pitcher that had performed as the ace of the staff in Seattle.

He found limited success, but he could not sustain any consistent winning streak. And for reasons far more significant than Langston's subpar outings, the Angels 1990 season became a bust. But to many, Langston, who finished the season with a 10-17 record and a 4.40 earned-run average, remained the focus of the team's failure.

"As I said, it was a year when I leaned on the Lord heavily. And He taught me. Baseball is not life and death," Langston says. "It really is meaningless in the bigger picture. But it is my job and the Lord wants us to work. You want to do your best and people are counting on you.

"So in that respect, it's hard to fail sometimes. That makes 1990 such a struggle in that way. But the Lord has shown me the way to understand it all. He's helped me see myself.

"What He wants is my best effort. That's what I've tried to keep giving no matter how the losses and disappointments others have tried to lay on me may mount. He wants my best effort. The Lord doesn't want me to snap and throw things and throw tantrums.

"I've been grateful for Him showing me that. It's brought peace in such tough times as that season. Because it was a very, very tough season."

Tantrums and other displays of bad temper were a regular part of Langston's persona on and off the playing field early in his career.

"Yeah, I've told people in the past that my real struggles are not with drinking or going to bars, but with my temper," he says. "I especially used to have a real nasty temper. I was a real poor loser. That's an area where the Lord has worked in my life."

And then Langston laughs. "Now, I've probably got the anger that rages down to five minutes after a defeat . . . I'm just kidding. Really.

"But I do continue to pray to the Lord to help me with it. He's already made me be able to handle it better. Believe me, it used to eat me alive. I kicked at everything and

broke things. That is how I handled things
that didn't go my way exactly." It is surely
the way he would have reacted to the
failures of 1990 before finding Christ in
1981.

"Yeah, I'm sure that's what some people
expected me to do when I was getting hit
and booed this time around," Langston
say.

He believes, in fact, that some of his
teammates or some California fans had
trouble understanding his peace in the
face of the adversities of 1990.

"Yes, I think some people might have
thought that way—been puzzled by my
peace—but I can only try to explain my
feelings," he says. "I can't be them. I think
if they understand that I want to win, that
I am trying my best every time, they will
understand."

Langston knows that, to some, baseball
convention demands boisterous displays
in such situations. Would fans have been
happier if Langston had heaved his glove
into the stands as he left the field after a
particularly tough loss as other pitchers
have?

"I don't think so," he says. "If you bring
your kid or your family to a game, you
don't want to see that. You don't want to
see a guy lose it on the field. You don't want
him to lose total control of his manners out

there. What does that tell your child?

"I wouldn't want my daughter seeing that. It is a family game. I think I'd want to see a player in control. Someone trying his best and not losing sight of that. I have to admit I wouldn't have seen it that way twelve years ago, but I see everything more clearly now anyway."

Langston became a Christian in 1981 during his first year of professional baseball, playing at the Class A, rookie level in Bellingham, Washington. He was a year from San Jose State, and as he says: "I was working the bars and drinking. Doing the whole nine yards.

"I really thought I was having a good time," Langston says. "Although looking back, I think even I knew I had to make some changes if I was going to be happy. I had started tapering off the wilder things in my life.

"My roommate in Bellingham and some of my teammates had been urging me to go to chapel with them. I went to chapel on Sundays and read from the Bible. I was still drinking and going out to bars and doing the whole scene at the time, but increasingly on Sundays I felt like I was missing the point.

"I really liked what I was seeing and hearing and what I saw and heard from other players and people in those Sunday gatherings. I wasn't unhappy with the rest of my life, but I was missing so much of what these people had it seemed to me.

"So I decided to take the next step. Not just go to chapel and read the Bible, but to commit myself to the Lord. I had to accept Him into my life. I don't want to make that sound like it was a simple thing. It is a big step, not one that you take lightly.

"But I needed to change some things in my life, that was obvious. And once I'd made the step, it's not like everything changed at once. It is a growing thing, being a Christian. You accept Christ as your Savior and you learn from what He shows you and where He leads you.

"It wasn't like 'bang' and it happened. For me it's been a procedure that takes years and years. It revolves and works as you reprogram yourself and your thoughts.

"Still, there was a point where I completely turned my back on those things. It may not have seemed as dramatic then, but when I reflect back on my life since, I know how I've grown and how much my life has improved.

"I have so much inner peace and a lot of joy in my life now. Everything has become different. The biggest thing is that I have a comfort of knowing that the Lord is in charge of my life and our lives. I know that I have accepted Him and that when it's all said and done, I know where I'm going. That's the number one thing. That brings enormous peace that nothing else on earth can bring.

"It happens when you read the Bible. It's all there. Just read it. You either believe in the Bible or you don't believe in the Bible. It's not an in-between thing. No one makes you a born-again Christian. The decision is left up to you on where you want to spend eternity.

"I read the Bible and know it is fact. It is not a fictional account. So I know where I'm going when this time on earth ends. That's a comforting feeling that I wish everyone could feel. I wish more people could come to understand it."

There was a time when Langston, like other Christian baseball players, felt the baseball community was anything but understanding about how he felt and believed. While with the Seattle Mariners, playing with several Christian teammates including All-Stars Phil Bradley and Alvin Davis, the team's management publicly questioned the Mariners' aggressiveness and intensity, pointing a finger at what they referred to as "too many laid-back religious types."

"But those days are gone," Langston says. "That was just a ridiculous period. Without a doubt, our beliefs are accepted now. It's not a big thing anymore. A lot of that has to do with what Baseball Chapel has done. We are people who are seen for what we believe, and I think other baseball players know that it's a commitment we've made that isn't going to be shaken. They can see our happiness, and I think many of them are curious about it, and at the least, happy for us."

One thing Langston still hears frequently in locker rooms across America are questions from newspaper reporters who want to know if the professional athlete's on-the-road, high-profile way of life makes it hard to maintain a Christian lifestyle.

"I just have to tell them that I don't believe that it's so," he says. "First of all, the Lord wouldn't put you into something you couldn't handle. He wouldn't put you in a situation that you couldn't handle through His guidance. So all anyone in their life has to do is ask for His help.

"Just because we're baseball players, that doesn't mean we have a way out of things. We must live our lives as the Bible says to as well as anyone else.

"Sure, if you want to get caught up in some of that stuff, you can. Certainly, people put baseball players on a pedestal. They like to hang around them and praise them and pump them up as bigger than life. But if you're a Christian, you don't allow yourself to be put in those situations.

"People say: 'But what about all the attention? Isn't it hard not to give in?' Not for me it isn't. I don't have any desires to go into bars or mess around. It's not even a focus of my life. I used to drink and go to the bars. I did all those things. But I know I shouldn't if I'm a Christian. I had to change all that. And I did.

"In 1981, I asked the Lord into my life. It may not have seemed as dramatic then, but when I reflect back on my life since, I know how I've grown and how much my life has improved.

"I've come so far. I know I've got miles and miles to go forward still, but the change has made me happy in a way that I never would have been happy. There are really no things in this life I would have accomplished without my commitment to the Lord. And it all goes back to 1981.

"You accept Him as the number one thing in your life and you read the Bible and it's obvious what things you have to clip from your life—like drinking and smoking and lives spent in bars.

"People ask me how I know to live this way and what I should or shouldn't do. They make it seem too hard, as if we have a rulebook that's part of an outside organization or something. Well, we do, sort of. It's the Bible. The Bible will tell you what to do. That's the foundation. It will lead you on a path that can bring you everything you could possibly desire."

As evidence, Langston points to his wife, Michelle, and daughter, Katie. To a renewed dedication to fulfill the rest of his contract with the California Angels. To trying his best to recapture the efforts that made him one of the best left-handed starting pitchers in the American League.

"I trust in the Lord and I will work for Him," Langston says "That will bring me all I need. I put it on the Lord and let the Lord lead me. It is like my plans for my life after I'm through playing baseball. Right now, I speak in the off-season to groups and try to help those that might need it.

"But what I will do when I'm done playing, I don't know specifically. I pray for the Lord's guidance on what to do with my life after this part of my job and work is done. I trust in Him. How could I not?

"Look at what he has done for me already. I married my wife in 1985. She is a Christian, too. I look at her and my daughter and know that other than the Lord, they are the best aspect of my life. My family is a complete joy. It is an example of the Lord working in my life. How can there not be a God in a world where we are given the gifts of life like a wife and a child?"

DARRYL
♦ Strawberry ♦
10

Few players in the modern era of New York baseball, and certainly no player in the thirty seasons of the New York Mets, stirred fan emotions and the cauldron of controversy as vigorously as Darryl Eugene Strawberry.

Born in Los Angeles a month before the Mets played their inaugural game in 1962, Strawberry was the first amateur player selected eighteen years later when the Mets, as the worst team in baseball, were granted the draft's top choice.

A day later, Strawberry, who had not yet graduated from high school, was posing for pictures in New York's Shea Stadium. They put him in right field for those pictures and team officials said the position belonged to him as soon as he was ready. The following day, for the first of hundreds of times, the New York tabloids used the headline: Strawberry Fields.

It sounded rosy, but the expectations were building on Strawberry's teenage shoulders. Everyone in New York knew that the eighteen year old from Los Angeles had received a signing bonus of $210,000, a sum so princely that the *Baseball Register* broke tradition and included it as a footnote to Strawberry's official biography.

And he had yet to swing in a paid at-bat.

Strawberry as a pro was not an immediate success, but by his third year in the minor leagues, he was leading the Class AA Texas League in home runs and was named its Most Valuable Player. By 1983, Strawberry had advanced to the big club, and in 122 games for the Mets, hit 26 homers and was named the National League's Rookie of the Year.

He was teamed with Dwight Gooden, the Mets magical young starting pitcher. Together, they were helping the Mets win the battle for the fans' attention in New York. Here were young stars like Strawberry and Gooden drawing fans away from the aging Yankees.

In 1984, Strawberry had another good season, leading the team in home runs and runs batted in. But statistically it was only slightly better than his rookie year, and somehow that wasn't enough to satisfy every Met fan, who noted that even with the new blood the Mets had still finished second—the franchise's eleventh consecutive season without a title.

In the spring of 1985, Strawberry, now twenty-five and feeling a veteran of the New York media wars, told reporters that he would carry the team to a championship. Strawberry had developed a persona of great bravado. "They can climb on my shoulders," Strawberry said that spring of his teammates.

It wasn't a popular remark, especially to several of the Mets true veterans, who found the comment a slight to their leadership roles.

Increasingly, Strawberry was becoming involved in the politics of the Mets clubhouse, where twenty-five professionals dress and ostensibly live for six months— while dozens of reporters record their every thought, musing, or outburst.

Strawberry had become known for his tantrums, his very late nights in nightclubs and bars across America, and, not surprisingly given his lifestyle, for his unpredictability. He was becoming a puzzle to management. Some days he smiled and seemed content. And occasionally, he hit the big home run.

But on so many other days, there was

trouble near the Strawberry locker. He showed up late for buses, planes, even the occasional ballgame. He criticized his teammates from time to time in the newspapers. Once on team picture day in spring training, a ritual akin to the first day of summer camp, he had to be restrained from trading blows with first baseman Keith Hernandez.

His performance at the plate was nearly as erratic, but Strawberry remained one of the most feared power hitters in baseball.

In 1986, the Mets had a dream season, defeating the Boston Red Sox to win the World Series in seven dramatic games. Strawberry played poorly, driving in just one run on a meaningless home run in game 5. He was even lifted from the climatic game. And few were surprised when Strawberry did not take it well.

Off the field, things were getting worse for Strawberry. He had a new contract and a championship ring, but tranquility remained elusive, to put it mildly. There were constant problems with his wife, Lisa. The couple endured separations, the embarrassment of a child Strawberry fathered by another woman in St. Louis, and, following the 1989 season, Strawberry's arrest after Lisa Strawberry alleged that Darryl drew a gun on her in their suburban Los Angeles home.

The charges were later dropped, but Strawberry was shaken enough to check himself into a treatment center for alcoholism. He emerged healthier, but not necessarily content.

In 1990, there was a new contract to negotiate, the talented Mets team was still not in first place, and Strawberry continued to chafe under the intense pressure of playing in New York, which he only made worse with his capricious comments to the media.

Strawberry would later call this time his "nightmare in hell." He says happiness eluded him at each of the many turns his young life had taken. "Nothing ever seemed right," he says now. "Through all the turns my life took, I know, and I always knew, that I was not finding happiness."

He fled New York the day the 1990 season ended, settling in a home in the Los Angeles suburb with his wife and two children.

He made a bold decision in November 1990, opting for a larger and lengthier contract offer from the Los Angeles Dodgers. His Mets experience over, Darryl was looking forward to playing at home in L.A.

The Dodgers are especially known for the family atmosphere they try to bring to their clubhouse, to their locker room, to the field. The ringleader is manager Tommy Lasorda, the man who would hug a traffic cop even as the officer scribbled a speeding ticket.

To be sure, there are players perfectly happy to be playing elsewhere in the major leagues, and many happy to have played for the Mets, which is an organization known for patience and stable management, but for Strawberry the change of scenery was an elixir. Most likely, it was just the lifting of the pressures burdening him in New York since he was labeled the eighteen-year-old Mets phenom, but whatever the cause, there was no doubting that Strawberry embraced everything in Dodger Blue.

"What you hear about the Dodgers is true," he says, several months after signing his new contract to play in Los Angeles. "It is like a family. And they treat their family well. You don't have criticism; you have support. The Dodgers are part of some of the good things that have happened to me. Of course, they are only a very small part of it. There are a lot of reasons why I now look and act happy. I have changed my life."

On January 6, 1991, Strawberry left his house with the uncle and godfather of his wife, Bill Payne, a retired officer with the Los Angeles Police Department. They attended an evangelistic crusade at the Anaheim Convention Center.

"You could say it was like I had been struck by lightning," Darryl says. "The power of God just came on and it struck me and knocked me off my feet. There are some things that some people won't believe, but I was there and it happened to me. When you go to the Lord, you're not looking for it. You go in there with an open heart. And that's what I did, I went in with an open heart. And I was receiving. And when you start receiving from the Lord, it's just the way the Lord works. He knows that's it's your time to come into the Kingdom and make a change in your life.

"I went there and before I knew it things started to happen in my life. I started receiving the Word, not with my mind but with my heart."

"That day in Anaheim, Darryl went out on his feet," Payne told the sports newspaper, *The National*. "He couldn't get up. When he finally did get up, I was standing there, staring at him. I knew he was clean of all the demons that had tormented him. I would stake my life that he'll never go down the wrong path again."

"My mother, Ruby, was a very religious person and she used to tell me that the Lord hears a cry for help," Strawberry says. "But I had to want help. The Lord has been watching me for along time. There were people who used to tell me I'd seek His help. Now I know it is true. Those demons of lust, anger, fear, and jealousy, they had me in their grip. My drinking was all a part of it, too. I asked for His help and He cast them aside.

"Hey, it's the best thing that ever happened to me. There are a lot of people out there with a lot of emptiness in them and they don't know why. And I can tell them why now because I lived it."

Strawberry's conversion became big news in the nation's sporting pages when he arrived at the Dodgers spring training camp in March 1991. Usually tardy for the opening of spring practice, Strawberry came early.

When reporters greeted him, he told them, "I'm free for the first time since I was a kid running in the playground. I'm free. I'm in a new world now. I accepted the Lord into my life and my life has just been full of happiness ever since I accepted the Lord. It's a blessing."

Strawberry's faith drew skepticism from some of his former teammates and from portions of the media. Strawberry says he expected it.

"It's not for me to try and convince someone, though I knew I would hear that reaction from some people," he says. "I know what I have so I don't really worry about what people say. I'm the one who has the personal relationship with the Lord. Those people are dealing with the natural. I'm no longer dealing with the natural. I'm dealing with what's inside of me.

"Personally, as people watch me now, I think they will finally realize that I wasn't fulfilled in New York. I was not whole. I was lacking and a sinner. The Lord is going to open a lot of doors for me in that way and people will get to know me and see me in a different light.

"I'm a happy man now. I wake up happy every day. I have no worries about anything. I look forward to every day. In the past, I woke up looking forward to a nightmare of hell. That's what it was. Every day.

"It affects everything I do. In my career, I always felt pressured, under the gun. Now I realize baseball is not pressure. It's fun. I've been set free of all that pressure and worry. Now, it's fun. Just do it. But my man upstairs has shown me that. That's the most important thing. That's who I listen to."

Howard Johnson was a teammate of Strawberry's on the Mets. Johnson accepted Christ into his life just a few months before his former teammate, but when he met Strawberry on the six occasions the Mets and Dodgers met in spring training in 1991, he was nonetheless struck by the transformation of the man he played and lived with for six years.

"Darryl had such bad problems with alcohol and women," Johnson says. "He hit bottom. But seeing Darryl now, talking to him now, seeing what he's been through, he's a changed man. It's a miracle."

Strawberry began the 1991 baseball season slowly, hitting just one home run in April. On his first trip to the East Coast to play, among other teams, the Mets, Strawberry's every move was followed by a gaggle of newspaper reporters and television crews. In a game in Philadelphia during that May trip, he struck out five times in five at-bats, and made an error in right field.

"What can I do or say?" Strawberry said after the game. "Last year or two years ago, I probably would have gone out and gotten drunk after a game like this. Tonight, I will go home and read the Bible. It has a lesson for everything, including when you fail. I will be back tomorrow and that's the best news."

And Strawberry took some criticism, if restrained, for his less-than-enraged reaction to a disappointing baseball performance that evening.

Said Strawberry's Dodgers teammate and fellow Christian, Orel Hershiser: "There will be times Darryl falls. They will write things about his personality or his actions on the field or off. He might not look like a Christian. But the one thing about Christianity, the reason you are a Christian, is you realize you need a Savior and you need forgiveness and you are not perfect."

"It's ridiculous when people say or think that I won't try as hard now because I'm a Christian," Strawberry says. "Hey, just watch me. That's all I can say. Just watch me. Becoming born again you get full of the Spirit of God, but that's just more glory for your life. It doesn't affect what I have to do on the field. It probably gives me more motivation. It's just how you handle it and how you go about what you have to do. My job is being a professional baseball player because that's what the Lord blessed me to do."

Four days after his poor game in Philadelphia, Strawberry returned to Shea Stadium for the first time since signing with the Dodgers. The newspaper headlines did not need to trumpet his arrival that day; Strawberry's return had been news for two days in advance.

His introduction at Shea Stadium brought boos from the grandstand. Standing near home plate, Strawberry doffed his cap and bowed from the waist.

Many in the crowd cheered. Strawberry smiled and bowed again. He made an out, and then another in his next at-bat. But in the sixth inning, he hit a home run to left-center field. There were still boos from the crowd, but the cheering nearly drowned them out.

Strawberry's home run helped ignite a Dodgers comeback that did not end until the ninth inning, when Strawberry entered the batter's box as the game's go-ahead run with two outs. He grounded out to end the game.

And afterward, while disappointed, Darryl Strawberry was composed. The scene did not jibe with the Strawberry so many had seen after losses at Shea in the previous eight years.

"I wanted to win; it's part of my job," Strawberry told the New York media. "But I'm not going to throw my bat and curse the world. That time is over for me. It's that simple."

Simple and direct, it was the new Darryl Strawberry. At 6-foot-6, 200 pounds, and with a swing that should earn him a place in Baseball's Hall of Fame someday, he will never blend into the crowd.

"But I am at peace with the crowd," he says. "And that is more important than it seems. I am not struggling to find my place in this world, on this earth. I am not concerned with pleasing the fans or my coaches. All this, baseball and prestigious things and money and house and cars, those things are irrelevant. They are meaningless to me. I have Jesus now and I know what I have after that. I know that I have a personal relationship with God and it's a relationship that is going to take me a long way.

"I have eternal life. That's more important to me, to understand how to live in Christ, than to worry what is happening on natural earth. I love my God. Nobody is going to take that away from me, because you can't. No one on this earth can.

"And there's such peace in that, it can't be described by someone who has never felt it. Baseball was always what I did well, the thing I found more effortless than anything else. But nothing is as easy as loving the Lord. And nothing could make me happier."

FRANK
◆ Tanana ◆
11

At twenty-four years old, Frank Tanana was the best left-handed pitcher in major league baseball. If you didn't think so, all you had to do was ask him.

"Nothing I do awes me," Tanana said in 1976. "I'm that good, that's all."

A year earlier when he led the American League in strikeouts he was asked about his idol growing up. Said Frank: "To tell you the truth, I didn't have an idol as a kid except myself."

That same season, on June 21, 1975, Tanana became the first left-hander to strike out 17 batters in one American League game. "I felt invincible," he said afterward.

By 1977, as the ace of the California Angels pitching staff, Tanana had been named to three All-Star teams and his blazing fastball had helped him win 82 games. His 2.54 earned-run average that year was the league's lowest. "I can carry a lot of burdens," he said. "Call it cockiness, confidence, or whatever, but I'm loaded with it."

And not only was Frank Tanana sure that he was as good as he said he was, to Frank, that's all that mattered. It was all that should have mattered to anyone.

Rummage through the library files chronicling Tanana's baseball career and you will also find this newspaper quote from Hall of Famer Frank Robinson, who managed one of Tanana's opponents, the Cleveland Indians: "Tanana will never be the pitcher he should be because he doesn't take care of himself. At the rate he's going, he won't last long."

Rummage through the memories and recollections of the now thirty-eight-year-old Frank Tanana, and you will find that he rues the days of what he calls "my huge ego," agrees with his old rival's appraisal, and most of all, is so very thankful that Frank Robinson's forecast was as accurate as it was.

Because late in 1977, Tanana strained a tendon in his million-dollar left elbow. Early the next season, he seriously injured his left shoulder. In baseball parlance, he blew out his arm. It wasn't just jargon. It usually carried a stunningly final diagnosis: Career over. Case closed.

Yet today, Tanana says this of his arm injuries: "They were the turning point in my life, and in many ways, the best thing that ever happened to me."

Tanana makes this statement from the breadth of a baseball career that entered its thirteenth "postinjury" season as a member of the Detroit Tigers in 1991. That's 403 games and 111 major league victories—and counting—since his fastball went dead.

But Tanana's good and positive notions about his arm injuries have nothing to do with baseball, except in the sense that the devastation he felt at the time brought him to question his values and priorities. Eventually, it brought him to a new life, to Christ.

And in a very genuine way, adversity, indeed injury, actually gave birth to a lasting baseball career.

But that is to digress. Not to mention how it ignores the true and natural course his life has taken. As Tanana says: "It has been just as they say: 'From darkness unto light.' "

Tanana was raised a Roman Catholic in Detroit, the son of a policeman. Athletics brought success and became his identity. As a pitcher at Detroit Catholic-Central

High School, he had an astounding 32-1 record. Though a month short of his twenty-first birthday, Tanana was the California Angels' first-round pick.

"I was really proud of myself," he says. "Pride was a big thing to me. I was boastful. Your basic loud-mouth."

By the time he was twenty-one, he had skipped through the minor leagues and had appeared in 43 games for the Angels. Already, he had established himself as one of the hardest throwers in baseball. Sports writers, meanwhile, were wearing themselves out trying to think of imaginative ways to rework an old sports cliché: Tanana played as hard off the field as on it.

It was his reputation and he regaled in it. "People say I live this 'bachelor lifestyle,' " Tanana told the *Los Angeles Times* in 1975. "If that means I go out and have fun every day, then I'm guilty. And loving it."

Told once that they were referring to him as "the Joe Namath of the West Coast," Tanana could not contain a wide-mouth smile. He was tall, tanned, and talented.

"I thought I was living the American Dream," he says. "I had it all, as they say. I was on the top of the world. And with that came all the success, the fame, the glory, the popularity, the financial reward. It was dizzying and I was enjoying it.

"I was having a great old time. I was

living a life of total pleasure. I had a big drinking problem. I drank all the time except when I was pitching, of course. Because the only other thing that mattered to me was baseball.

"I had a lust problem, too. There was baseball and other than that, sexual gratification was my main objective. Eventually, I paid a deep price for this lifestyle. Because of the off-the-field activities, I practically ruined my career. I practically wrecked my arm forever in 1977 and '78. My career was in real trouble.

"At about the same time, I married my wife, Cathy, and I heard the Gospel for the first time. In a sense, the story of my coming to Christ is in two parts. But this was the beginning. I had been thinking that I wanted to make some changes in my life. I knew I couldn't continue like this."

Tanana had suddenly, and painfully, become an average pitcher in the dwindling days of the 1978 season. "I began to question myself: 'What after baseball?' I really didn't have anything. If you took away that ball from me, you'd take everything from me."

But Tanana was to be troubled by far more tragic events than a debilitated arm. In September 1978, on a road trip to Chicago, his Angels teammate and friend Lyman Bostock had been an innocent victim of a shooting incident on a city street. Bostock was killed as he rode in a car with a group of friends, felled by a shotgun blast intended for someone else.

"Lyman's death had a profound impact," Tanana says. "The suddenness of it. The reality of dying. I asked myself the question: 'What if someone shot at me? Where would I spend eternity?'

"I started thinking and wondering if I shouldn't be searching for something more. Cathy had started to go to a Bible study in the off-season, and she had asked me if I wanted to come along.

"I said: 'Sure, why not?' I enjoyed it and in the fall of 1978, that was the time when Cathy came to Christ. I too began calling myself a Christian. My understanding at the time was that I could do that. That all I had to do was believe.

"Still being the con man that I was, I thought it was too good to be true. I remember thinking: 'Is this all I have to do? Just say I believe and I'll be saved? I will go to heaven?'

"It seemed so simple. I had been brought up in church and had gone regularly every Sunday. My attitude was that I was a Christian. But always, always, I felt three things about this 'belief' in my attitude: (1) I wouldn't speak for Him; (2) I wasn't going to give Him my money; and

(3) I wasn't going to go to Africa.

"Well, you know, I couldn't have been more off-base. You don't cut deals with God. I was hell-bound thinking that way. What I was doing was living my own ideas. It was Frank's theology. Frank's Christianity.

"Still, I went to Bible studies and I read the Bible, but I had no real interest in it. Cathy and I had a family and we were getting along great, but I had no desire for the Word. I read it, but I didn't understand it. I called myself a Christian, but I was kind of mousy about it. I had begun to be less concerned with me, less self-centered, less selfish, but I was not committed to Christ.

"Finally in 1983, I went to a Pro Athletes Outreach conference. At one point, we were discussing the Spirit-filled Christian in a booklet they distributed. It described how he leads others to Christ, how he trusts God, and obeys God. How the fruits of the Spirit are love, joy, faithfulness, compassion, self-control. So many things.

"As I was reading this and listening to this, I became scared to death. I became convicted. I said to myself: Not only are none of those traits in your life, Frank, but they never have been.

"That's a terrible thing—to never have had these experiences in your life.

"I remember the day like it was yester-day. It was November 6, 1983. I got down on my knees and for the first time I took to heart that I was a sinner. That because of my sins, hell was my fate and I deserved it.

"But at the same time, I knew that be-cause of Jesus Christ dying on the cross, because Jesus Christ had taken my pun-ishment, I could be forgiven and saved and go to heaven. It was the first time I asked to be forgiven for my sins. The first time I committed my life to Him."

His commitment complete, Tanana saw the world with new eyes.

"What a dramatic change it made in my life!" he says. "What a wonderful change. I read the Bible now and understand it. I love reading it. It is part of my daily walk. Through God's power, I was able to end my terrible, alcoholic drinking. He has given me the strength to overcome that desire and others. I am able to keep my thoughts and avoid the lust that drove me in the past. I am faithful to one woman, my wife. That was not possible without His power.

"I love His Word and I love obeying Him. I owe Him everything. So much else changed, too. My church going took on a new meaning and experience. I saw other believers as close to me, closer than my own flesh and blood. I was part of a true family. All of His promises have been fulfilled."

At the same time, Frank was trying to rebuild his career—learning new pitches, learning, in fact, to pitch not just to throw. His fastball could no longer bail him out of any situation. Accepting Christ only made his career goals that much easier to reach.

"First of all, I could look at my work entirely differently," he says. "It wasn't a means for my own gratification. Colossians 3:23 says: 'Whatever you do, work at it with all your heart, as working for the Lord, not for men' (NIV).

"That verse sets the statement for work. That verse removes the pressure from me. I don't have to worry. Regardless of the score, all I have to do is my very best and I serve the Lord Christ. That's not to say that I don't play to win, because I do. I play to excel and winning is a lot more fun than losing. But losing is not the end of the world. I work to be the best.

"And now, my work habits are so much better. I am in better shape at thirty-eight than I was at twenty-two. It is all through His guidance and through His Word. Without Christ, my career would have been over years ago. I would never have been able to survive the adversity and the losing teams. My new attitude is God's gift.

"Without Him, I could not have handled the injuries and some of the bad years I've had that any athlete is going to have. I would have done something tragic or said something dumb because before coming to Christ, I was a hot-tempered, angry kid.

"Look at how I handled my very career. When you pitch in the major leagues, even when you're in top shape, there's a lot of pain involved. There is tremendous muscle soreness and you must go through a lot to be able to recover in time to make your next start.

"Alcohol retards the recovery process and worsens the stiffness and pain. When I was drinking, my recovery time was too long for a lot of reasons. Let's face it, you can't stay up all night and expect to pitch major league baseball. Yes, I did it for two or three years, but it caught up with me and I paid a dear price.

"Without Christ, I would have never rebounded or survived as a major league pitcher. And now I enjoy my teammates and see them as people. I can like them and enjoy them whether they do well for me or not. I used to look at them as a means to my end; they could help me get what I wanted.

"So in every way, coming to Christ has had a profound and dramatic effect on my career."

In the last decade, Tanana has seen the influence and presence of the Christian athlete mushroom in the athletic community. The acceptance is greater.

"I think we have to be thankful for Baseball Chapel for some of that," he says. "It has become a part of the game. If for nothing else, it is a chance to gather the Christians on the team and the many others who are interested, to spend a short time with the Gospel. I wouldn't miss it.

"And on a team, and in the clubhouse, I have found that if a man will walk his talk, if his life will back up his word, an athlete has no problem with that. If you love Christ and know Christ loves through you, and you are not judgmental and acting as the world's judge and jury, you will have no problems.

"You may not be understood and you may be laughed at or mocked, but only until you live your life and prove what you believe. Then there will be no problem."

Still, Tanana has seen some in baseball's management positions chafe at the behavior of some Christian players. He has heard the discussions of a backlash. It produces some strong opinions.

"A lot of Christians bring this problem on themselves," he says. "They don't understand the Word or they don't take the time to understand the Word. The ballpark is not the place to be telling someone about Jesus Christ. The ballpark is the place to play baseball. It's the place to shine for His glory.

"And you do that by running your laps and taking the extra hitting practice and shagging the fly balls. It's the place to concentrate on your game, your work. If it comes up in a casual conversation, that's fine.

"But you're asking for trouble if you make it too much a part of your workplace unless you show them that you're there to work hard as a baseball player, too.

"I've always felt the Christian athlete had to work harder and be better than the nonbeliever to have any kind of credibility at all. I know some people will not agree with me, but to me, the killer for the Christian athlete is the foolish statement occasionally made: 'It was God's will that I dropped that ball' or 'It was God's will that we lost.'

"Or when a player who is in a slump, instead of being seen out on the field taking extra hitting or working on his fielding or his delivery or something, is seen sitting by his locker reading the Bible.

"There is a time and place for that. Knowing the right time and place is called wisdom. And if you're a baseball player, you can advance Christ's Kingdom by being more wise in your evangelism. You're going to have your bad days, but your attitude can make a very big difference. I learned that the real problems in your baseball career will come when you shirk your responsibilities as a major league athlete. So sometimes, I can understand management's viewpoint. The ballpark is for my work and I'm paid by the Detroit Tigers.

"It's all in the Lord's way. He wants you to work and to be the best you can be at your work. And if the Lord's will so compels you to help someone, take them out to lunch. Go eyeball-to-eyeball in a neutral setting."

Tanana finds himself spending many of his off-the-field moments visiting churches in the Detroit area and talking to civic and men's groups.

"I take a couple dozen speaking engagements a year," he says. "It's an opportunity to share the Gospel."

He also attends the Fellowship of Christian Athletes meetings and the Pro Athletes Outreach conference every fall.

Living in suburban Detroit, Tanana says he tries not to travel in baseball's off-season. "You've got to remember that I have four daughters who see little of their father during the season, and I miss them dearly in this life on the road," he says. "They need me, as I need them. In the off-season, I want to do the best I can for them."

A far loftier goal than those he set at twenty-four years old. But this Frank Tanana tries to be the best he can be. And if you don't think so, all you have to do is ask him.

ANDY

◆ Van Slyke ◆

12

It was a summer scene of serene beauty: sailboats dotting the bay, a lengthy pier reaching toward the horizon until it seemed to disappear into the sea. Andy Van Slyke stared across the vista, standing in his baseball uniform on the well-manicured diamond of pristine Al Lang Stadium in St. Petersburg, Florida.

The bay breeze was warm, the waters calm, but Van Slyke was anything but composed as he shifted his position so that he stood on the field's home plate. Quiet and calm had not brought Van Slyke to this spot at this point in his life. It had been quite the opposite.

Some ninety minutes earlier, Van Slyke, a member of the St. Louis Cardinals Class A minor league team in St. Petersburg, had just played another game in the out-

field of Lang Stadium. When the game had
ended, he had retreated to the team's locker
room and waited for the grandstand to
empty.

The traffic dispersed as the grounds crew
watered the field and covered it for the
night. The concessionaires counted their
earnings and closed their service windows.

In the home clubhouse, Van Slyke waited
without a word. The stadium workers
locked the entrance gates and left. His
teammates showered, dressed, and, wav-
ing goodbyes to Van Slyke as he sat near
his locker, departed for the players' park-
ing lot. Van Slyke heard their car engines
start, heard the noise of their engines fade
until he knew he was alone in the ballpark
that had become his home away from home.

It was the summer of 1981, Van Slyke's
third year as a professional baseball player.
Twenty-one years distant from his birth in
Utica, New York.

"I went onto the field, I walked to home
plate, and I prayed," Van Slyke says, looking back at the decade-old event. "It was
something that I felt I had to do on a
baseball field. Baseball had been everything to me and at the time, I needed to do
it right where I had been doing all my
worshiping in all those days before this
one.

"So I waited for everyone to leave and I

went out and I stood alone at home plate and I said: 'I'm not going to let this game be more important to me than Jesus Christ.' And I gave my life to Christ. I put my trust in Him. I said that I was basically a cesspool. I was twenty-one years old and didn't know what Christ had done for me.

"I prayed. I'm not sure what I prayed except that I know I wanted to say that I never wanted the game to be bigger than Jesus Christ. I realized my sinful nature. He had died for all the terrible things I'd done and will do. I had understood it before but never trusted in Him completely, never trusted in what He had done for me. Right then, there was salvation for me."

Van Slyke, now the All-Star center fielder of the Pittsburgh Pirates, recalls the story with the delightful smile that marks his disposition. To him, there is a special joy in this ten-year-old story, and not just for the many personal and professional successes he has enjoyed since.

"It was the moment that I really started liking myself," he says. "I like myself because I know God loves me, because I know my wife loves me and my kids love me. With this, I have to know I am a little bit OK."

In fact, Van Slyke is one of the most popular players in big league baseball—with his teammates and opposing players, with the media, and with the fans. Unselfish with his advice to younger players, an example for his work ethic, Van Slyke is also community-oriented and one of the most quoted players in the game.

Win or lose, Van Slyke is the one reporters covering the Pirates seek for the comment that will lend perspective to the contest. "Oh, they just talk to me because they know I might tell a joke ," he says.

Like the time he was asked what person he would most like to be stranded with on a desert island. Said Van Slyke: "Marlon Perkins, the guy who hosted that TV show, 'Wild Kingdom.' "

Why?

"Because he would be able to tell me which animals I could eat, and which animals I could be eaten by. Big difference."

Or, the time he was asked what kind of third baseman he was as a young minor leaguer.

"Well, they wanted me to play like Brooks," Van Slyke responded, apparently referring to Baseball Hall of Fame third baseman Brooks Robinson.

"So I did play like Brooks." Van Slyke continued. "Mel Brooks."

Asked to recall that comment, Van Slyke laughs. "I think for me, I just got to the point where I was able to joke about my playing and my shortcomings because

Christ helped me rearrange my priorities," he says. "It goes back to everything I have been able to accomplish since I asked Him into my life in 1981."

Jokes about his playing abilities might not have set well with the younger Van Slyke. "I had a pretty bad temper when I failed back then," he says. "God helped me control that. And naturally, I find my thinking is more clear. I can concentrate on what's important. I may still get angry, but my blood pressure doesn't rise to heart attack levels. I am certainly not to the point where I sin now. My anger used to be unchained. It contributed to my attitude. And it did nothing but hurt me."

You can see it in Van Slyke's earliest statistics as a pro baseball player. As St. Louis's first-round pick in 1979 and the sixth player taken nationally, much was expected of Van Slyke. He sat out his first season with a hand injury, and after two years at the lowest rungs of the Cardinals minor league system, Van Slyke was hitting a paltry .242.

He was accustomed to being the star in his scholastic years, the center of attention for the athletic world of upstate New York. Now, playing in small towns in North Carolina and Florida, Van Slyke was just another failing minor leaguer. Another kid used to being the big fish in the small pond who was drowning in the ocean of talent that is professional baseball.

"Everything was going wrong," he says. "It wasn't just baseball, though it affected my baseball career greatly. I was partying hard, living like a mustang. I thought those were all the things the Lord was telling me to do and it was going to make me happy. It really wasn't."

And the temper in the face of the turmoil was unrestrained.

"He was a baby, throwing fits all over the place," Van Slyke's wife, Lauri, who began dating Andy in 1979, told the *Sporting News* in 1989. "He'd be going crazy on the umpires, getting in their faces. Everything you can imagine about a temper, he had it. He'd throw his bat, kick dirt, yell at everyone in sight."

At about the same time, some of Van Slyke's teammates approached him about attending the Sunday chapel meetings they had been conducting.

"I think it's important to note that I already considered myself a Christian," Van Slyke says. "I was raised in a family that went to church every Sunday. My mother was particularly insistent that I be baptized and active in the various church programs. I did it all. I thought I knew what was important to my salvation. I always figured that my good outdid my evil. And that was enough.

"But frankly, I knew that my life off the field wasn't very good. Baseball wasn't going really well, either. It wasn't satisfying me. So these teammates asked me to come to chapel with them. Again, I figured I was a Christian. But there was something different about them. Something in their mannerisms and in their eyes that separated them from me. I could see it.

"I had never been to Baseball Chapel, but one day because it was a Sunday, I went. If it had been a Wednesday, I probably wouldn't have gone. That's the way I thought then. I went in and listened to the guy leading the meeting, and I thought he was an absolute lunatic.

"He was very energetic. He was animated about the Bible and Christ. He was laughing and smiling. I had never heard someone talk about God this way, talk about Christ in such glowing terms. I was just stunned. I thought they needed a straight-jacket for the guy.

"Still something was appealing. There was something intriguing. It was strange how uncomfortable he made me.

"The next Sunday the same guys asked me if I wanted to go to chapel again. I said, 'Only if that guy isn't coming from last week.' "

And Van Slyke laughs. It is something he

does almost as well as play baseball. But in this case, this story, he knows he is only laughing at himself.

"The same guy was leading the session," he says. "And I thought about staying away. But you know, I couldn't stay away. Eventually, I slipped in there and I had the Bible presented to me for the first time really. It planted the seed of salvation. It was frightening in a sense because it struck me that I wasn't going to have personal salvation based on behavior patterns.

"I knew then that I had to do more. That I had to accept Christ as my Savior."

But there was a period where Andy only considered his options. "I was thinking," he says. "But I'm not stupid. Even then, I knew there were things in my life that I wasn't proud of. They're things I wouldn't want my kids to do. The time came though when I had to give my life to Christ. I knew it that night when I waited after the game and went out to home plate alone, asking for His help."

Van Slyke calls the first few months following his conversion his days as all "SSC."

"You know what an SSC is, right?" he asks "It's a Secret Service Christian. That was me. I knew what was going on in my life, how it had changed, but I didn't want others to know. I didn't go around banging on doors or anything.

"Obviously, there were big changes, though. My desire to stay up and party and smoke pot and try to find girls late at night changed. To say that I stopped immediately would be a lie, but I came to understand what I had to do, what had to be done. It was God's Holy Spirit that made that change, that made me see things differently.

"I had the desire to live a Christian life and to walk with God. Without that act, my lifestyle was going to undo me in more ways than one. It certainly was not helping my baseball career. It was only giving me problems. Afterwards, my whole perspective on the game changed. Up until then, my whole identity as a person was wrapped up in baseball and what I did on the field. My priorities changed. I started being properly focused. And I find it kind of ironic that I had been having no success as a pro before, and after that act in 1981, I have held great success."

There is no other way to describe Van Slyke's baseball career than as a great success. After parts of four seasons in St. Louis, he was traded to Pittsburgh in 1987 and truly blossomed as the Pirates center fielder, where he has since won three Gold Gloves, emblematic of the league's top fielder at his position. Batting in the middle of the Pittsburgh lineup, Van Slyke has produced in a number of ways, helping to lead the Pirates to their first division title in eleven years in 1990.

A career .270 hitter, Van Slyke had his best season in 1988 when he was a National League All-Star, led the league in triples with 15, and hit 25 home runs while driving in 100.

"I have been able to do all the things I was trying to do professionally, and it all turned on that night in 1981," he says.

Lauri Van Slyke adds: "And his temper is much, much better. Now he can strike out twelve times in a row, and he's frustrated but he has a handle on it. He doesn't take it out on me and the three kids."

His trade to Pittsburgh didn't seem to hurt, either. Things always seemed strained somehow in St. Louis, where manager Whitey Herzog once said of Van Slyke: "With Andy, what you see is what you get." It wasn't meant to be a compliment.

Now Van Slyke looks back philosophically. "I have no doubt in my mind that God wanted me in Pittsburgh," he says. "Whitey Herzog was but a tool to God's will. I'm where God wants me now. I really admired Whitey's abilities but we all, in some ways, suppress our abilities, not only in relationships, but in doing our jobs, too. I got to

Pittsburgh and I really worked on getting the most out of myself. I tried to do it every day, every inning, concentrate on playing hard, to be as good as I could. I wasn't asking to be perfect. I was asking God's help to be my water purifier."

His success has brought back-to-back, long-term contracts from the Pirates, though Van Slyke has never renegotiated or demanded a raise. "Personally, the money enforces my commitment to do my best in my work," says Van Slyke, who has chided other major leaguers who have attempted to renegotiate their contracts. "Money has never changed my attitude and I'm determined to see that it never does. I feel obligated not only to God and myself, but also to the ball club to be the same player I have always been."

His Christian beliefs, Van Slyke says, have never been viewed as anything but a positive by his employers.

"There isn't a thing about being a Christian that can be a drawback for a major league player," he says. "Not to mention all the benefits. But truthfully, in ten years, I've had only one or two incidents."

Van Slyke is aware of the national attention that then-Minnesota Twins third baseman Gary Gaetti received in 1989 because of his conversion to Christianity. Some of Gaetti's teammates chafed at

Gaetti's new life and his eagerness to talk of it.

"In my opinion, Gary was trying to run before he was ready to sit with God," Van Slyke says. "You have to sit with God before you walk with Him. One of the problems with Christians and Christian athletes is that we expect these prominent athletes to do too much publicly too soon. It was twelve years before Paul did his public ministry. Why should anyone expect a pro athlete to give his public ministry after two weeks?"

Van Slyke sees baseball as his life's work, though not always in the same venue that has brought him his success to date. "God has allowed this game to give me so much," he says. "But you can't just take from it. I'd like to give something back. I have a few dreams that way. Maybe not at the major league or minor league level, but at the adolescent level.

"God gave me a gift to play baseball. I don't deny that gift. He saved me on a baseball field ten years ago. But baseball is only something I do well. There are more extraordinary things we can do on this earth. I've always said that if you can keep the attention of fifteen five year olds for three hours, you have some special gift.

"I'd like to give back to the game that way. Being a good baseball player is one thing, but it isn't as extraordinary as being good at something like being a teacher."

But why at the adolescent level?

Andy Van Slyke smiles the smile he smiles a hundred times a day and says: "Because that's where dreams start. I want to be a part of that."

Bill Pennington is a sports columnist for *The Record* and *The News Tribune,* a New Jersey newspaper chain with a circulation exceeding 300,000. He has been selected by the Associated Press Sports Editors as one of the country's best columnists four times and twice took first place in their national writing contest.

Pennington, a Boston University graduate, began writing sports in 1979 and formerly worked at *The Providence* (R.I.) *Journal-Bulletin* and *The Stamford* (Conn.) *Advocate.* He has been published in *The Sporting News* annual, *Best Sports Stories,* several times and contributes to a number of sports publications.

Bill lives with his wife, Joyce, in Warwick, New York.